Step-by-Step
PICTURE FRAMING

Step-by-Step
PICTURE FRAMING

A COMPLETE GUIDE
WITH CREATIVE PROJECTS

Tom Winkworth &
Susan Berry

Photography by Michael Crockett

WEIDENFELD AND NICOLSON
LONDON

First published in 1996 by
George Weidenfeld & Nicolson
The Orion Publishing Group
Orion House
5 Upper St Martin's Lane
London WC2H 9EA

British Library Catalogue-in-Publication Data
A catalogue record for this book is available from the British Library

ISBN: 0 297 83547 5

Created and produced by
Phoebus Editions Ltd
Studio 19
10-11 Archer Street
London W1V 7HG

Editor: Emma Callery
Designer: Carol McCleeve
Stylist: Leeann Mackenzie

Printed and bound in Italy

CONTENTS

FOREWORD
by Tom Winkworth

For a quarter of a century I have been involved in the picture framing business, and it seems hard to believe that my involvement started when I was framing pictures in the back room of my home. My business has grown since then and we now have a retail gallery and import machinery from America and the Continent. We also have a trade counter supplying all framing needs for professional and hobby framers.

Along the way, I have been down the road of mass-produced pictures for major retail outlets, but still get the most satisfaction where I can treat each piece of artwork with the individual care and attention that it deserves. I also see that people have an insatiable desire to learn and I get a lot of pleasure in disseminating some of the experience that I have gained over the years through the professional framing courses, basic framing and mount decoration workshops that I run.

I feel that if you look around your home you will find any number of items to frame. This ranges from the obvious, such as pictures and photographs, to the not-so-obvious which would not usually be considered for framing, such as collectables and mementoes. These can easily be accommodated in box frames. I would rather have them displayed in a frame than hidden away in a drawer. This book demonstrates a variety of techniques to allow you to achieve this. For no more than the cost of having a couple of pictures framed by a commercial framer you can purchase all the materials and equipment you need to get started.

On my travels to America and Europe I have seen a wide variety of framing techniques used. I am particularly enthusiastic about mount decoration techniques such as wash lines, marbled paper and stencilling. I hope that once you have seen how effective they are you will share my enthusiasm.

A thought on looking after your artwork. Increasingly I am becoming aware of the need to use framing techniques and materials, such as acid-free mount card, to preserve our heritage from the ravages of the environment such as pollution and insects. I would encourage you to do the same.

Finally, I hope that you enjoy using this book as much as I have enjoyed working on it. Happy framing.

Charisma Picture Framing, July 1996

Introduction

It is well known to anyone who paints, draws or takes photographs that the way in which you frame the image makes a huge difference to the appeal of the finished picture. It can turn a simple piece of work into something special, simply by focusing attention rather more acutely on a single aspect of it.

As much an art as a science, picture framing makes special demands on all those who seek to master the craft. Not only do you need to be capable of precise and accurate cutting and measuring, you also need an eye for form and colour. This is because you have to create a visual whole with the image to be framed, any mount (or mat) you may use, and the moulding from which the frame is eventually made.

When beginning to frame your pictures, it is important to take a good look at other framed images – in galleries, other people's houses, museums – wherever there are pictures hanging. You will soon see that there is an exceptionally wide range of images that can be framed, and also many different ways in which they can be framed successfully.

Initially, it can be quite daunting to make decisions as to the final size, colour and shape of both the moulding (the outer, retaining, element of the frame, usually of wood) and the mount (the card that protects the image from contamination by the glass, and which provides an inner frame).

Take heart from the fact that even the experts disagree among themselves about the best colour or width of mount to use, and the style or form of the frame. Fashions change in framing as much as in anything else, and what may have been considered attractive and smart a few years ago might have less appeal today. However, that said, it is not a good idea to go overboard for modern innovations in framing, as ideally you expect the frames to last for some time, and you do not necessarily want to change them every time fashions change. If in doubt, go for the classical approach every time.

Throughout the book, the framing techniques use a variety of images – photographs, hand-tinted photographs, oil paintings, drawings, embroidery and even pressed flowers – to give you as wide a range as possible as well as different mount and frame styles. Although the choice of frames and mounts has already been made for these by us, you are not obliged to copy our ideas too slavishly. Rules are made to be broken, and although these pictures have been professionally framed, there are often other, equally successful, solutions that you could adopt.

The Practicalities of Framing

If you are interested in picture framing, it probably stems from an interest in at least one of the visual arts, possibly several, either as one who practises it or as a collector. Either way, you are almost certainly going to want to frame quite a large number of images, and it is therefore important to decide in advance what kind of equipment you might buy.

There is a great deal of equipment for picture framing at your disposal which you can buy, or possibly hire. It ranges from the very simplest hand-held equipment to precision calibrated machinery which would require a small mortgage to purchase.

When setting out, you do not need more than fairly basic tools and materials (see pages 18-19). It is important, however, to find a good supplier from whom you can purchase all the equipment and materials you will need. Later, if you become more seriously interested in framing, you can order direct from the manufacturers yourself.

This book has been organized to give you a short course at the outset in basic framing. It goes on to provide information and instructions on more advanced techniques and equipment, as well as some ideas for more inspirational, rather less technical, framing finishes.

Setting up as a Framer

In the first instance, you could obtain the very simplest and easiest equipment, a hand-held mount cutter and a combined mitre box and saw for cutting mouldings – as given in the details on basic equipment on pages 18-19. If you decide to carry on, then you may think of spending a bit more money and purchasing a more advanced mount cutting machine, which actually makes the job easier than the hand-held version. If you can afford to, go straight to the more advanced mount cutter anyway – you can always sell it if picture framing does not turn out to be your forte!

Although this book is organized as a basic course, from which you will be able to master the essential techniques of framing, it can be extremely valuable to attend a course in framing as well. This is particularly helpful when it comes to some of the more advanced aspects of framing such as cutting variously shaped mounts, for example. You can find several organizations that often offer day or short courses, which may prove invaluable.

Of course, if you find that you enjoy picture framing and have a knack for it, there is nothing to stop you turning it into a full-time career. However, be warned that in order to charge competitive rates you have to be extremely deft at what you do, and you will also need to equip yourself with professional, high-quality equipment.

IMAGES TO BE FRAMED

The style of images you may wish to frame can vary enormously, ranging from postcards and prints to photographs, drawings, textiles and oil paintings.

The aim is to show off the image to best advantage – here are just a few of the images we framed in this book, using a variety of different mounting and framing techniques and styles. In each case, the aim was to enhance the picture by looking not only at the style and subject of the image, but the kind of paper it is executed on and its condition and form. The hand-tinted photograph of the little girl is shown on page 69, the penguin on pages 21 and 27, the bowl of quinces on page 51, and the sepia family photograph on page 65.

Judging Mounts (Mats)

Most images benefit greatly from being displayed with a mount, and this can take two forms. Either the mount encloses the image, the central aperture providing a frame for it, or the image is float-mounted (laid directly on top of the mount) so that while it provides a border, you see the edges of the image.

To some degree, the kind of mounting you choose depends on the image you are framing. But, in general, if the image's edges are integral to its aesthetic value, then float-mount it rather than cut a mount to fit. For example, a drawing on cartridge paper with a hand-made edge is better float-mounted (see pages 112-13). However, a watercolour that is imprecisely positioned on the paper on which it is painted would be better framed with a specially cut mount – either a single or a double.

When cutting mounts, you need to make certain preliminary choices. You have to pick an appropriate form of mount card, decide on the right size, and choose a colour that tones with the image.

There are several different kinds of mount card which come in both plain and textured surfaces. The most commonly used are standard mount card (made of approximately six sheets of pressed card bonded together), museum card (which is acid-free and is used for precious works of art so that they do not get damaged), and mount core board, which is backed with another colour that shows through when it is cut, creating a contrasting effect.

CHOOSING A MOUNT CARD COLOUR

It can be difficult to make the right choice of mount colour, and no two people are likely to be in complete agreement as to the choice. However, there are certain rules and guidelines which can be helpful. It is normally wisest to pick one of the colours in the image, but remember that this will accentuate one colour in the image and cause others to recede. You need to be aware of this when choosing the mount colour, so pick several shades, all of them representing different colours in the image, and then try them against the image to see what kind of effect each one has upon it. You may find, for example, that picking out the distant blue of a mountain range brings the foreground colours into sharper focus. Alternatively, picking out a single, but quite dominant, colour in the painting can immediately focus your attention on this particular part.

Here a traditional watercolour is the central image (shown framed on page 12). In order to assess the colour and type of mount for it, you need to examine a range of possibilities. Different coloured mount cards will bring out different colours and elements within the image; a defining gold or contrasting line close to the image will give it a crisper, more professional finish, for example, and a contrasting double mount a more subtle emphasis.

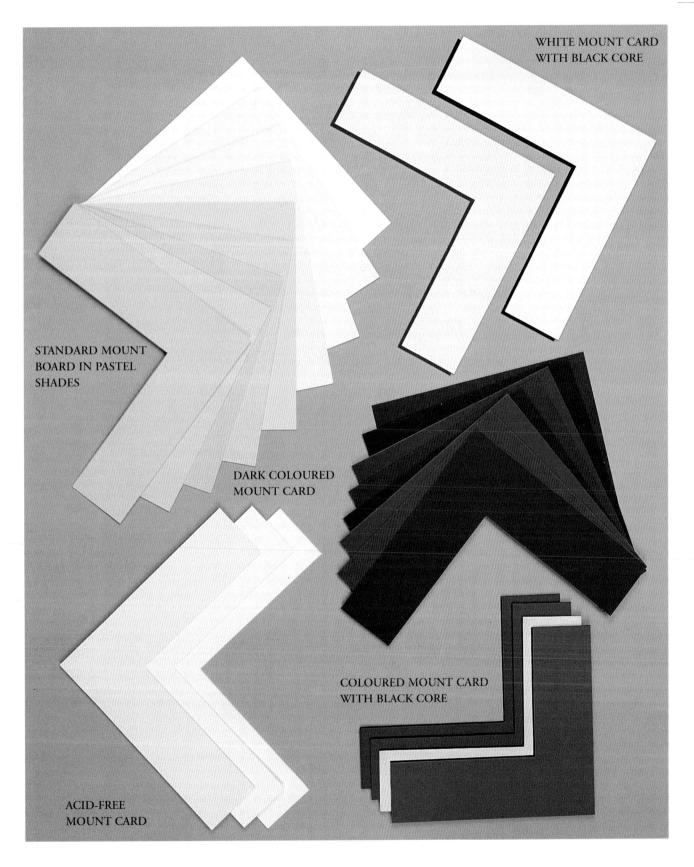

WHITE MOUNT CARD
WITH BLACK CORE

STANDARD MOUNT
BOARD IN PASTEL
SHADES

DARK COLOURED
MOUNT CARD

COLOURED MOUNT CARD
WITH BLACK CORE

ACID-FREE
MOUNT CARD

Types of Mount Card

Mount card comes in a range of types, thicknesses and colours. An example of the range is shown here. These include ordinary thickness, standard mount card, core board (which is two-coloured, so that when the top colour is cut away the secondary colour is revealed), acid-free card for conservation purposes, and coloured mount card for creating contrasting coloured under mounts.

Here the final colour of mount chosen for the framed image of the watercolour was
a toning off-white top mount, with a sage green under mount, the latter picking
out the more dominant green in the painting itself.

Judging Frames

As with mount cards, there is a very wide range of colours, materials and forms of mouldings from which to make a selection. You will also have to decide on an appropriate width of moulding. It is important to remember that the width of the moulding will affect the finished look of the mount as it alters the balance of the image as a whole.

Mouldings are mainly made from wood, although you can also buy metal (normally aluminium) mouldings as well, which come in either the natural aluminium colour or in painted, coloured finishes. If you opt for an aluminium moulding, get it cut to size when you order it, as you cannot cut it on a mitre saw used for wooden mouldings. (Instructions are given on pages 110-13 for assembling aluminium frames.)

There is such a wide variety of wooden mouldings to choose from that sometimes it can be hard to know what type and form to select. On page 14 we show examples of some of the most popular forms, but bear in mind that you can also create your own finishes and decorations for the moulding, as discussed in the chapter on decorating frames.

In general, look for a moulding that blends harmoniously with the image you plan to frame so that it neither swamps it nor does it look too meagre. Not only must the size be appropriate, but also the form of the moulding should match the style of the image. For example, a modern piece of embroidery would look completely wrong if given an ornate, gilded frame appropriate for an oil painting. By and large, the simpler the image, the simpler the frame. It does not automatically follow, however, that a large image needs a large frame, or vice versa. A big poster, for example, will often look best with a narrow aluminium frame, while a small watercolour may well be enhanced by a wide frame, perhaps stained and limed in a toning colour.

The question of aesthetic balance is a hard one to tackle, since much depends on the eye of the beholder. Only by trying various mouldings against the image and the chosen shade of mount card can you really tell if they enhance the image, or quarrel with it.

Choosing the right colour and weight of moulding for the frame can be quite taxing. You need to be aware of certain effects: a very heavy, wide frame can dominate the central image, and a very light, pale one may fail to give the image a sufficiently defined boundary. If in doubt, err on the side of caution, and pick a modest width in a restrained colour: enhance the image, don't overwhelm it. Try holding different corner mouldings against the mounted image to see which works best. Four different but equally acceptable mouldings for a watercolour of flowers are shown here: a wider, green stained frame with a narrow gilded inner border (left, bottom), a more traditional narrow moulding, again with a gold edge (left, top), a purplish stained narrow moulding with a narrow gilded inner border (far left, bottom) and a wider, plain, natural pine frame (far left, top).

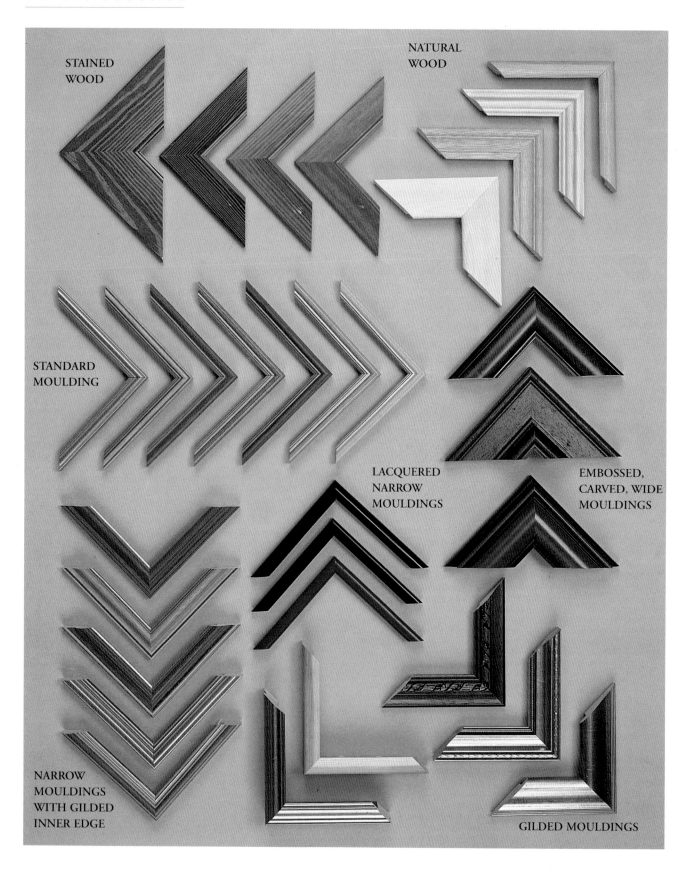

STAINED
WOOD

NATURAL
WOOD

STANDARD
MOULDING

LACQUERED
NARROW
MOULDINGS

EMBOSSED,
CARVED, WIDE
MOULDINGS

NARROW
MOULDINGS
WITH GILDED
INNER EDGE

GILDED MOULDINGS

TYPES OF MOULDING

The range and style of mouldings used to make the frame is enormously varied, with a range of different woods, finishes, widths and decorative forms to the moulding. Popular finishes are gesso (a matt paint), staining (which reveals the texture of the wood while colouring it) and gilding (which can be done with gold, silver or copper finishes). The style and type of moulding you choose will be determined by the kind of image you are framing – for example, a large, traditional oil painting might well look best with a traditional carved gilded frame, a poster with a modern, narrow metal one. Those shown here are all variations of wooden mouldings.

A traditional narrow moulding with a gilded inner edge was chosen for the final frame for this watercolour of a vase of flowers. The dark colour of the wood creates a defining border, while the touch of gold lifts and lightens the overall effect.

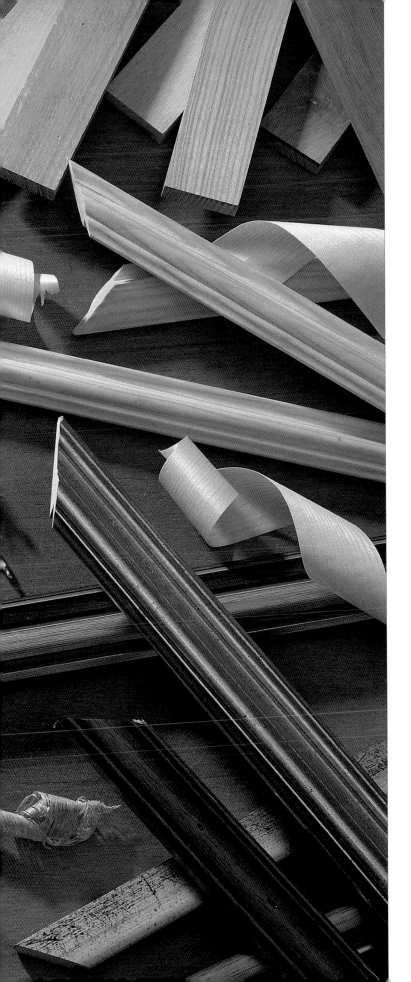

Chapter One
BASIC FRAMING

This section shows you the techniques and equipment required to make a basic picture frame, including a single and double mount cut on the most basic hand-held cutter; how to measure, cut and assemble a frame; cut glass; and, finally, how to assemble the image and mount in the frame. The elements of framing are not particularly difficult to master, provided you take accurate measurements and make your cuts precise, as these are crucial to final success. While the techniques are comparatively elementary, the precision needed is that of a professional, so practise on surplus pieces of card, moulding or glass to ensure that you can carry them out with ease.

Basic Equipment

When you are setting up as a picture framer, you will need to decide what kind of equipment to purchase in the first instance. This is a difficult decision, since some of the best equipment is extremely expensive. Fortunately, it is perfectly possible to frame successfully with relatively basic equipment, and a starter kit is shown opposite.

If you are unsure as to the eventual number of frames you are likely to make, you may well not want to splash out on some of the most expensive, state-of-the-art machinery. First and foremost, you will need mount cutting and moulding cutting equipment. For cutting mounts, you can begin with a very simple hand-held Cushway cutter (see page 20), perhaps progressing to a more expensive Logan compact cutter (see page 48) once you are sure that you will continue with the craft. To cut mouldings efficiently and precisely, you will find that a combined mitre box and saw (see page 30) is essential, while not being prohibitively expensive.

CARE OF EQUIPMENT
Carefully store all tools and materials in labelled drawers, shelves or boxes. Make sure any sharp tools are kept away from children, and ensure, too, that all blades are wrapped. To obtain properly professional results, the tools you use must be clean and sharp. For example, the blades of saws should be changed at regular intervals to ensure that they are sharp. Likewise, glass-cutting tools must be kept in a jar with a rag moistened with white spirit and oil to keep them sharp. Make sure all caps and tops are replaced after use. When you have finished work, safely dispose of all debris, in particular taking care that shards of glass are swept up.

WORKING AREA
In addition to the appropriate tools, you also need a place to work which is well lit, ideally with an adjustable lamp over the area where you will be working. You will also need a solid workbench of a good size (much depends on the size and scale of the images you are likely to be framing). If possible, the bench should be freestanding so that you can walk around it. If your workbench has shelves underneath it, this will be the ideal place to store some of the equipment but, if not, you will need to provide some storage space.

If you can build a special unit to hold some of the larger, more unwieldy materials, such as glass sheets or mount boards, so much the better, as it is very easy to bend or damage the mount card or break the glass. Although a horizontal shelving unit, such as an architect's plan chest, could be used for the card, a storage unit with suitably sized vertical slots is needed for large sheets of glass. For a work surface when cutting glass, you could use a large board, covered with a piece of smooth carpet, placed on top of an existing table.

Once you have framed your pictures, make sure that you stack them safely until they are hung. Stack them vertically to prevent the glass breaking and use corner covers to protect the mouldings (see page 45).

THE ESSENTIALS

For Mount Cutting
A basic hand-held cutter (such as the Cushway cutter initially), progressing to the more expensive Logan compact cutter (see page 48), measuring tape, craft knife and metal straightedge with a non-slip rubber backing.

For Cutting Mouldings
A combined mitre box and saw; lengths of moulding.

For Mount Decoration
Whatever tools are required by the style of mount decoration you intend to employ. Popular decorative devices such as wash lines require watercolours, brushes, corner-marking devices and a straightedge; for ruled lines, you will need a ruling pen.

For Glass Cutting
A glass cutting tool and straightedge. Glass gloves are useful to prevent you cutting your hands when carrying glass.

For Assembling the Frame
A backing board, D-rings, bradawl, hammer, straightedge, craft knife, wire, string, Framemaster and gummed paper tape.

In addition to the above list, you will also need the usual miscellaneous equipment of pencil, eraser and scissors, plus, of course, picture hanging equipment, such as hooks, etc.

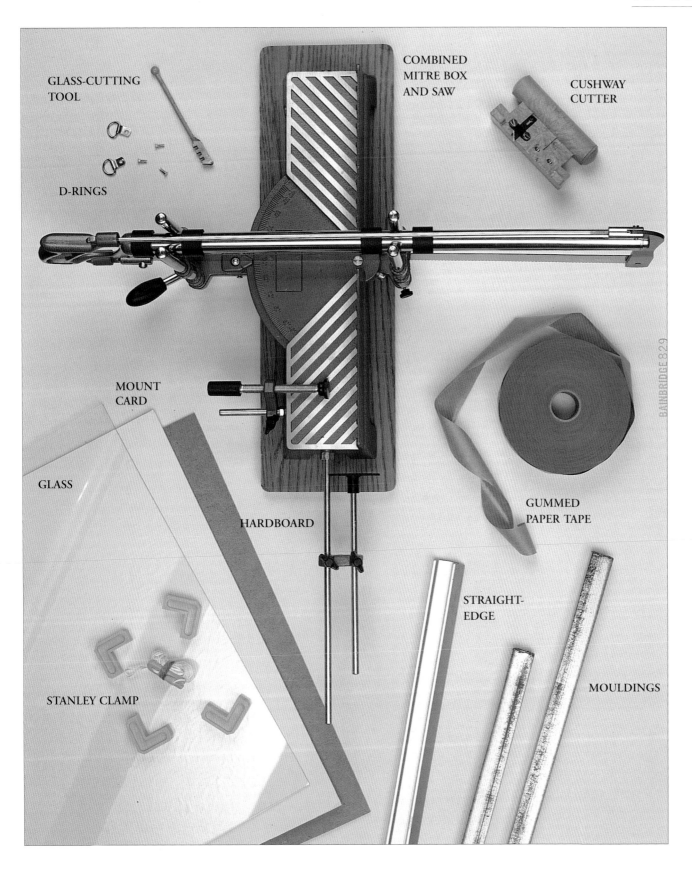

GLASS-CUTTING TOOL

COMBINED MITRE BOX AND SAW

CUSHWAY CUTTER

D-RINGS

MOUNT CARD

GLASS

HARDBOARD

GUMMED PAPER TAPE

STRAIGHT-EDGE

MOULDINGS

STANLEY CLAMP

BAINBRIDGE 829

Basic Equipment

The equipment shown here forms the basis for any picture framer, which you can add to as you become more experienced at the craft. If you can afford it, instead of the hand-held Cushway cutter, top right of picture, go for the Logan compact cutter shown on page 48, since it will produce a professional result more easily. The combined mitre box and saw (the most expensive piece of equipment shown here) is essential; do not be tempted to economize and get a very basic mitre box. You will find it impossible to cut accurate mitres for the mouldings with it.

Cutting a Single Mount

This is the simplest form of mount, involving a single sheet of mount card and a single aperture for the image. To cut it accurately to size, you will need to use the appropriate equipment – in this case a hand-held Cushway cutter and a rubber-backed straightedge or a Maped cutter, which fits on to its own ruler.

To produce a professional result, not only must the mount be cut accurately, with neat corners, but it must frame the image successfully, the border of the mount being neither too wide nor too narrow. Before you begin, choose a suitable type and colour of mount card to go with your image (see pages 10-12) and assemble the materials you will need (see below). For a relatively strong image, such as the simple black and white print of a penguin featured opposite and overleaf, a single mount in toning white card looks appropriate, setting off the image well and concentrating the eye on it. Equally successful, however, would be a double mount, using black mount card to create a very narrow border or slip (see pages 26-9).

Accurate measuring and precision cutting are vital for a professional result, so check and double check the measurements before you cut, and take great care when cutting the mount card to follow the aperture markings precisely. You also need to ensure you exert an even, steady pressure on the cutter, and it is well worth practising on some old bits of card first to check that you can cut clean, straight lines.

If you are going to position the finished picture high on the wall, consider making the bottom border of the mount deeper than the other borders. It gives the image better proportions as, when seen at higher levels, the bottom border can look narrower than it actually is. If you decide to do this, cut the template for the lower border slightly wider and mark the aperture accordingly.

If you cut a few sample templates from spare mount card, you can use these to gauge possible widths, placing them next to the image to be framed, which is easier than judging widths entirely by measurements. It is very easy to get the calculations wrong, even if you are an accomplished mathematician, so *double check* your figures before you cut the mount card. You will first need to measure the height and width of the image to be framed. Then, to decide the overall size of the piece of mount card needed, you will need to add the desired width of the borders to this for the height (x 2) and for the width (x 2). Step-by-step instructions are provided on pages 22-3 and these are followed by instructions for using a simple hand-held cutter on page 25.

Checklist

Measuring tape

Pencil

Mount card

Templates for borders

Rubber-backed metal straightedge

Craft knife

Cushway or Maped cutter

CUSHWAY
CUTTER

PENCIL

MEASURING
TAPE

RUBBER-BACKED
METAL STRAIGHTEDGE

MOUNT
CARD

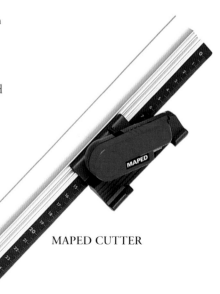

MAPED CUTTER

The framed single-mounted image of the penguin has a single, toning mount in off-white card positioned to reveal the narrow, fine box rule around the black and white print. The size of the borders is fairly generous to give the overall image a feeling of solidity. A plain, narrow, black moulding completes the effect.

MEASURING UP

Your first task is to calculate the size of the borders you need for your single mount. There are no real rules as to an appropriate size but, generally speaking, a border about 3 to 8cm (1¼ to 3in) is acceptable. For certain effects, to give more substance to a small drawing, a much wider border is sometimes used. Err on the side of generosity, as a very narrow border can look mean and unattractive.

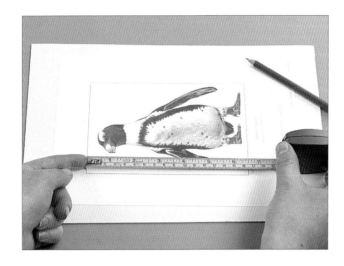

1 To gauge the size of the aperture, measure the height and width of the image accurately. In this case, the image has a fine rule around it, and this is used as the measuring guide for the mount card. Get into the habit of measuring the longest side first and then measure the shorter side.

2 Write down the measurements on a spare piece of card and add 2mm/⅟₁₆in to each measurement for a cutting allowance. To ensure the fine rule around the drawing is visible, a further 2mm/⅟₁₆in is added to each measurement.

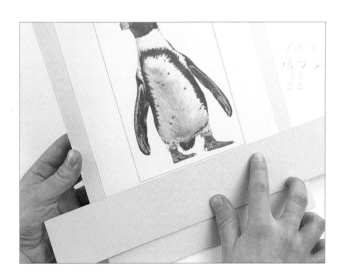

3 To give the overall size for the mount card, assess the width of the border, using a template as a gauge to help you judge the right size, and then add the width of the border (x2) to the aperture width measurements and the width of the border (x2) to the aperture depth measurements.

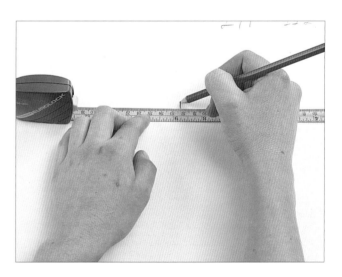

4 Mark out the overall dimensions on the mount card, taking care to use it as economically as possible. This will determine the overall size of the mount card.

CUTTING THE MOUNT AND APERTURE

5 To cut the mount card to size, using the straightedge and craft knife, score the board lightly first all the way down one cutting line. Cut once, cut twice and then cut all the way through on the last cut. Repeat this procedure on the other sides to cut the mount card to the overall dimensions required.

6 To mark the aperture on the mount card, line up the border template with one edge of the mount card. Using the straightedge butted up against the outer edge of the template to hold it in place, rule down the inner edge of the template to mark one side of the aperture. Repeat around the three remaining edges of the card until you have drawn each of the aperture markings.

TIP *For a professional result, accurate measuring and precision cutting are vital. So check and double check the measurements before you cut, and take great care when cutting the board not to over-run the marked aperture, thereby creating unsightly overcuts in the corners of the aperture. You also need to exert an even, steady pressure on the cutter. It is well worth practising on some old bits of card to ensure that you can cut clean, straight lines.*

ASSEMBLING A CUSHWAY CUTTER

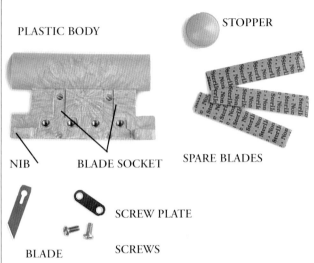

PLASTIC BODY

STOPPER

SPARE BLADES

NIB

BLADE SOCKET

SCREW PLATE

BLADE

SCREWS

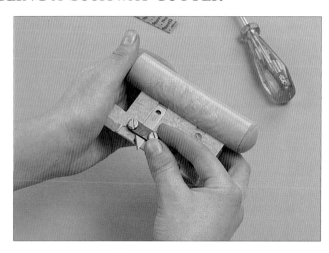

1 Insert the blade and adjust the screws by hand to get the blade in the right position, For right-hand use, have the diagonal part of the blade facing away from you on the cutter.

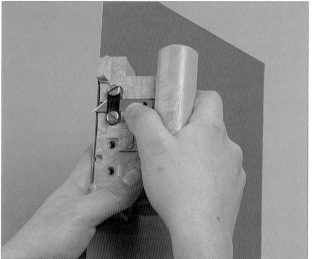

2 Test the blade against the mount board to position the tip so that it is just far enough down to cut through the board.

The Cushway cutter is a simple, hand-held cutting instrument, which consists of a sharp blade fixed at a 30-degree angle to a plastic body, and a grippable handle. You use it with the blade side of the body towards you, and the angled edge of the blade facing away from you in the slot furthest from you. There are two slots for the blade in the cutter, so that the blade can be inserted into the machine for either right- or left-handed use. The Cushway cutter is used in conjunction with a straightedge and is not difficult to operate, but, when assembling the cutter, take care you position the blade depth correctly. The aim is to get it to cut neatly through the card, but not through the cutting surface beneath. You will need a screwdriver to tighten the screws that hold the blades in place on the body. Spare blades are kept in the handle.

N.B. When using the cutter, the **nib** is on the cutting line, the **blade** 2mm/¹⁄₁₆in within it.

FOR LEFT-HANDED USE

To assemble the Cushway cutter for left-handed use, remove the blades, holding plate and screws, and insert them in the other socket, ensuring that the angled edge of the blade is forwards when the blade side of the cutter is facing you.

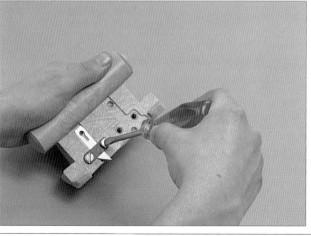

3 Using a screwdriver, tighten up the screws to fix the blade in position. (You must screw these up really tight or the blade will work loose.)

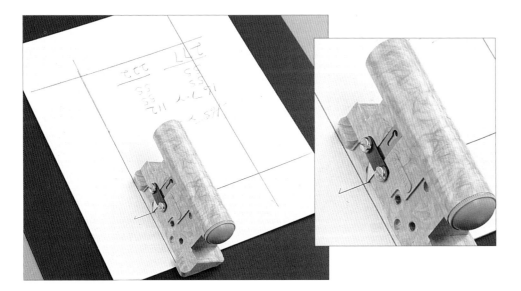

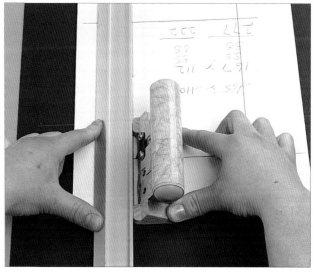

7 Align the cutter with the nib on the vertical left-hand aperture cutting line and the tip of the blade on the horizontal aperture cutting line. In the detail, the nib of the cutter is on the vertical cutting line, and the blade is 2mm/1/16in inside this line, with the tip of the blade on the bottom horizontal cutting line. (Your aperture will therefore be cut 2mm/1/16in smaller than than the marked line, which is why the allowance is required.)

8 Line up the straightedge with one edge on the vertical aperture line. Use both hands, pressing the straightedge and the cutter together to ensure that they are both accurately lined up and lying firmly against each other.

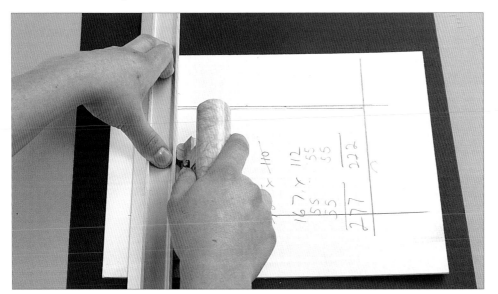

9 Cut the aperture by pushing the cutter down and forwards to the upper horizontal line, exerting equal pressure on both cutter and straightedge and cutting in one continuous movement. When you reach the pencil marking line for the next side of the aperture, stop the cutter with the tip of the blade just on the line.

10 Cut the remaining three sides in the same way, and then lift the card to allow the aperture to drop out. If the aperture does not drop out, you have not cut right through; turn it over and use a craft knife blade to ease it out.

Cutting a Double Mount

This double mount is cut using a hand-held Cushway cutter, as was used for the single mount on page 25, and with the same central image – the penguin. You have already cut the single mount; now you are aiming to create an under mount which will reveal a narrow contrasting border, inside the aperture of the single mount.

To create a double mount, you need two pieces of mount card: a top mount and an under mount. Apertures will need to be cut in each to reveal a narrow (normally about 5mm/³⁄₁₆in wide) border of the under mount when the two cards are placed on top of each other. Usually, contrasting colours are used for the mount cards for this kind of effect, but occasionally the same colour card is used for both mounts, giving a toning finish. A greater width of contrasting border can be used but, generally speaking, the effect is smarter if the contrasting border is fairly narrow, particularly for relatively small images.

In general, a neutral card is used for the top mount and a deeper, toning colour, for the under mount. Pick one of the main colours from the image for the under mount, and echo the background colour of the image for the top mount.

Although it is perfectly possible to cut a double mount simply by using measurements, templates are useful as they save any possible confusion over the mathematics of the measurements, especially when using a simple cutting tool like the Cushway cutter shown here. Two templates are needed for a double mount – one for the under mount (as shown on pages 20-5) and a slightly narrower one (5mm/³⁄₁₆in narrower) for cutting the top mount. Later, if you use a more elaborate cutting tool, such as the Logan compact cutter shown on page 48 which can be set to certain measured widths, you can work with measurements alone and dispense with templates. The techniques for measuring and cutting are just the same as those for cutting a single mount.

Checklist

Measuring tape

Pencil

Mount cards (here in contrasting colours)

Border templates

Cushway cutter

Straightedge

Double-sided tape

Craft knife

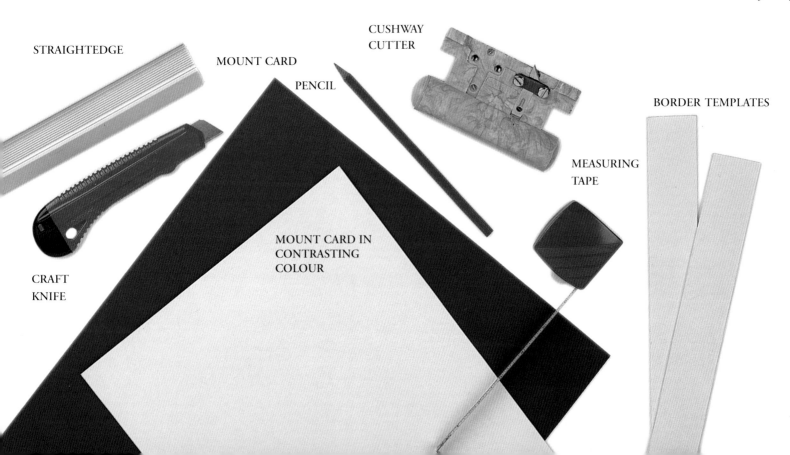

STRAIGHTEDGE

MOUNT CARD

PENCIL

CUSHWAY CUTTER

BORDER TEMPLATES

MEASURING TAPE

MOUNT CARD IN CONTRASTING COLOUR

CRAFT KNIFE

Here the central image of the penguin has been double mounted by giving it a contrasting inner mount to create a narrow black border within the existing single mount shown on page 21. The addition of this inner mount helps to give the overall image a crisper, more finished, appearance.

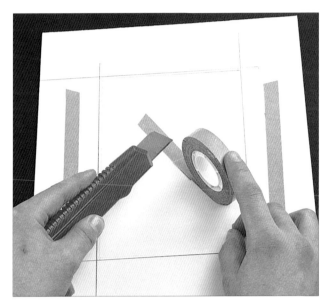

1 Cut the top mount to the overall dimensions required for the image (see page 22). Then cut the card which forms the under mount so that it is slightly smaller than the top mount – by about 10 mm/⅜in in height and width. (N.B. The under mount card is black with a white reverse side.)

2 Take the top mount and, using the narrower template, cut the aperture to the required dimensions (see page 25) but do not remove it. Tape the back with double-sided tape as shown above and then lay the under mount, face down, on the back of the top mount.

3 Working with both top mount and under mount face down, position the 5mm/¾in wider under mount template so that its outer edge is against the outer edge of the top mount. Draw along the template to mark the aperture, repeating on each side of the mount. This marks the cutting area for the aperture for the under mount.

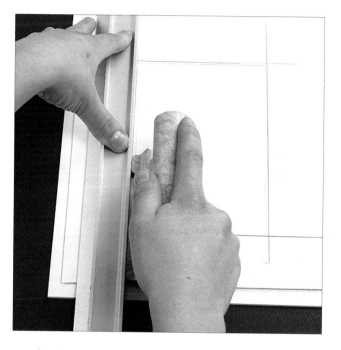

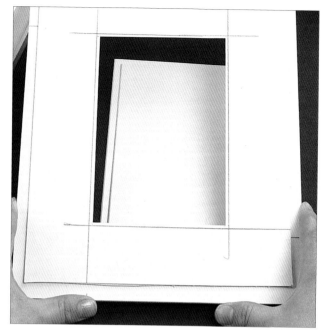

TIP *Ideally, you should not stop while cutting a line. But if you do have to move the position of your hand on the straightedge, stop cutting while you do so, release the pressure on both hands, and begin again without moving the Cushway cutter.*

4 Line up the straightedge along the ruled lines and cut the aperture for the under mount in the same way as you did for the single mount (see page 25).

5 Lift the mounts off, and the aperture, if correctly cut, will fall away, revealing the double mount. (If it doesn't drop out, take the tape off, turn the mount over and ease it out with a craft knife – see page 25.)

MAKING A TRIPLE MOUNT

You can make a third under mount to reveal a second contrasting colour. Proceed as for a double mount, then cut the third mount card and piggy-back it as for the double mount card. A narrow grey border (to the same 5mm/³⁄₁₆in width as the black one) has been used as the third mount for the picture on the right, and a wider border for the mount on the far right.

Cutting a Moulding

The next stage in the framing process is to cut the mouldings to the size required for the frame. The choice of style of moulding is one of personal taste, but it is easier to cut relatively simple styles of mouldings, as those with flat edges can be more easily held in position.

The accurate cutting to length of the mouldings is a key part of the framing process. It is not particularly difficult, but it does require patient attention to detail, and an ability to measure accurately, since the frame will not be square unless the pieces of moulding are the exact lengths required – the smallest mistake can throw the mitre joints out of true, and prevent the frame from being a perfect rectangle.

To cut mouldings accurately, you need a combined mitre box and saw (right), in which the saw is mounted on the mitre box. Although it is possible to cut mouldings using a separate mitre box and a hand-held saw, it is far more difficult to do the job accurately as the box has no stops.

PARTS OF THE MITRE BOX AND SAW

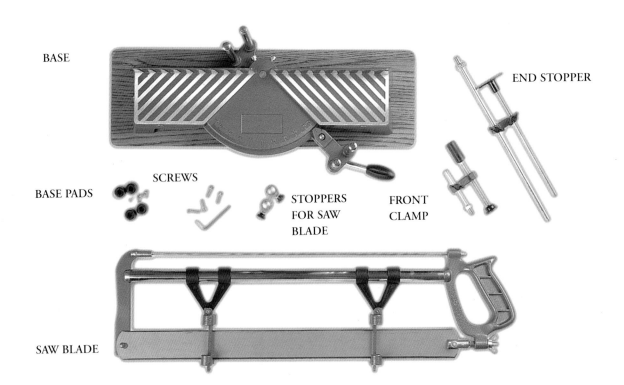

BASE

SCREWS

BASE PADS

STOPPERS FOR SAW BLADE

FRONT CLAMP

END STOPPER

SAW BLADE

The combined mitre box and saw for cutting mouldings is featured above, It comes in kit form and its component parts are shown to the left. It has a base to which the saw is screwed down; clamps to hold the moulding; stoppers that keep the moulding in place; and the saw, which pivots on a central axis with a lever that allows you to swing the saw around to make left- and right-angled mitre cuts in the mouldings. It is important to maintain the saw properly: to ensure that the blades are sharp, replace them regularly.

ASSEMBLING A MITRE BOX AND SAW

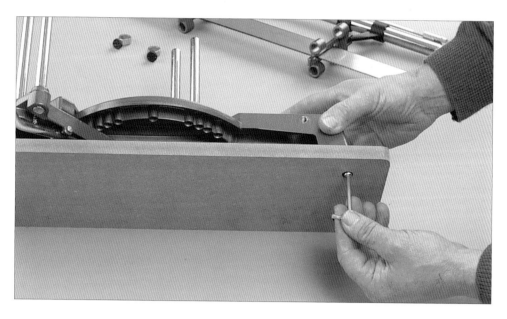

1 Screw the wooden base to the mitre box to hold it firmly in position.
You will need to turn the base and mitre box on their sides to do so.

2 Put in the clamps by screwing them into the
appropriate holes in the front edge of the mitre box.
Then tighten the nuts with an adjustable spanner or
a pair of pliers.

3 Put the stop that determines the cutting length for
the moulding into position on the supporting unit,
by screwing it in, and then sliding it into place.

TIP *When using the mitre box, clamp it to your workbench to prevent any movement while sawing. You can purchase the clamp from any good hardware store.*

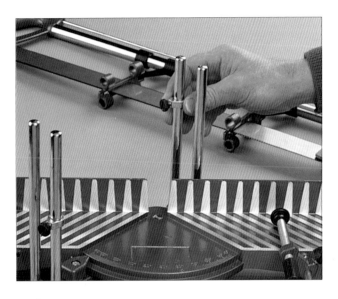

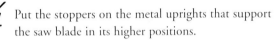

4 Put the stoppers on the metal uprights that support the saw blade in its higher positions.

5 Lower the blade onto the metal uprights so that the sockets on either side of the saw slot onto them.

MAINTAINING YOUR MITRE SAW

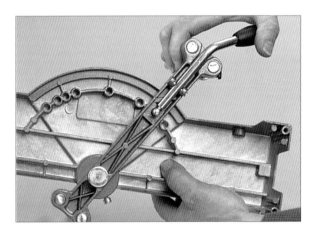

With use, you may find that the adjusters for the saw start to work loose. You can tighten these at the back of the box using an Allen key. Tighten them enough to make the saw reasonably firm but not so tight that you are unable to adjust its position.

When positioning the saw, you must be able to slot it into the locating holes on the base of the machine. If you keep the spring in the locating pin oiled (as well as any other moving parts of the saw), it will make your work easier.

Cutting the Mitres

Once you have chosen the appropriate kind of moulding for the image you intend to frame, you can set about measuring and cutting them to make up the finished frame.

Mouldings (see page 14) come in a whole range of types and sizes, but for the purpose of measuring and cutting, it is the inside edge of the moulding (known as the rebate or rabbet) that is used as the measuring guide.

Always cut the longest lengths first because if you make a mistake, you can then use these for the shorter sides. Never rush the cutting of a moulding; do the job methodically and systematically, to avoid making mistakes.

Hold the moulding firmly in place before sawing. When using the saw, aim to move it backwards and forwards in short, steady movements as this will create a less grainy finish on the sawn wood.

After cutting the first mitre, there is no need to measure the moulding again to cut the second mitre. If you are using the combined mitre box and saw shown here, and have put the stop in place (in step 6), you do not need to measure the moulding again as the stop indicates the correct length of the moulding once you have inserted it in the mitre box. You can then cut the second mitre, confident that it is in the right place.

1 Measure the image, with any accompanying mount, and note down the height and width measurements to determine the overall measurements for the mouldings.

HARDBOARD
(TO CREATE SAWING
GUIDELINE)

PEN

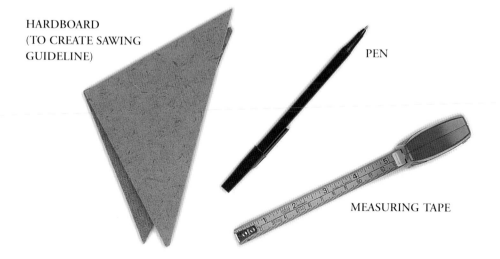

MEASURING TAPE

MOULDINGS

Checklist

Measuring tape

Pen

Combined mitre box and saw

Mouldings

Hardboard (to create sawing guideline)

You will need to cut two opposite angled mitres (a left- and right-hand) at the end of each moulding, each at a 45-degree angle, so that they make a perfect join when the two sides are put together. It is essential to cut these mitres accurately to the required measurements, otherwise the frame will not be square, and will not fit together properly. If one of the mouldings is longer than the other, recut the second moulding to match the first. Cut the right-hand mitre in each moulding first, followed by the left-hand mitre.

2 To cut the first right-hand mitre, take a length of moulding, put it in the left-hand side of the mitre box with the rebate facing you. Pack the hollow part of the mitre box with one or two triangular pieces of hardboard. Check the saw is at 45 degrees and cut using a steady movement.

3 To cut the second (left-hand) mitre, remove the moulding and swivel the saw to the opposite 45-degree angle.

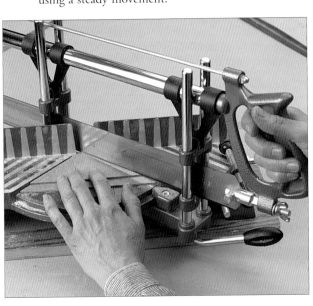

4 When the saw is in the right position, mark the hardboard triangle with a saw line. This line will form a cutting guide for steps 6-8

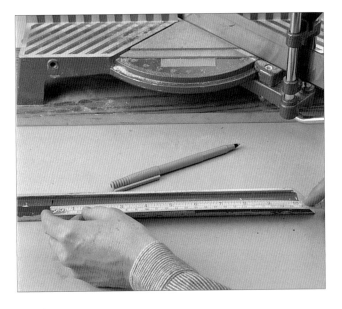

5 Measure the required length of the moulding along the inner edge of the rebate and add 2mm/¹⁄₁₆in for ease. Mark this point on the rebate.

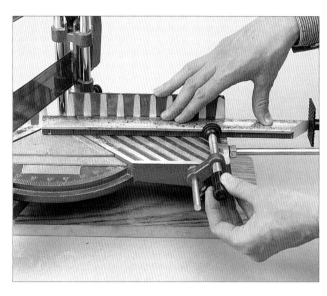

6 Insert the moulding from the right of the mitre box, rebate towards you, and line it up so the marked line on the rebate for the left-hand mitre cut is just to the right of the marked saw line on the hardboard triangle. Push the stop on the right to mark this position.

7 With the moulding correctly positioned, clamp it in place. Hold the moulding firm with one hand, making sure the stop is against the end of the moulding, and turn the clamp with the other.

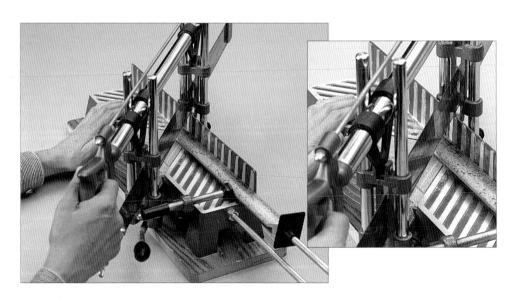

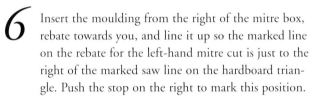

8 With your left hand steadying the moulding, make the second cut with the saw, using the same smooth, light movements.

9 Cut the matching moulding to the same measurements (the position of the stop will determine the cut length), and then hold them back to back to see that both pieces are identical. Cut the other pair of mouldings in the same way.

Assembling the Mouldings

Once you have successfully cut the mouldings to the correct measurements, you can begin to assemble the frame by gluing the four pieces of moulding together, held in a clamp or vice so that the joints do not separate. There are several different kinds of clamp you can purchase, but the Stanley clamp (used here) is one of the simplest. It consists of four plastic corner pieces, a cord and a tightening device.

To stick the mouldings together, use any proprietary wood glue. However, you must ensure that it is dry before removing the clamp and hammering nails through the corner joints to fix them.

If, for any reason, you have failed to cut the mouldings so that they are the same length, you will have to re-cut them, or the frame will not be square.

It is important to fix the nails so that they are at right-angles to the vertical side of the picture. If you nail them vertically down through the joints, rather than horizontally, the weight of the picture may cause them to come apart.

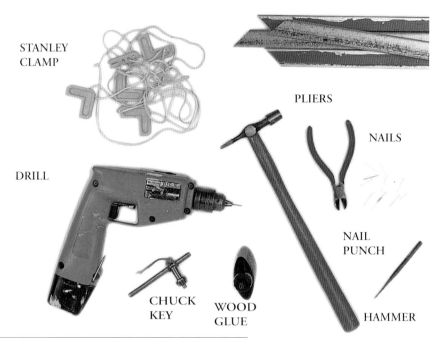

MOULDINGS

STANLEY CLAMP

PLIERS

NAILS

DRILL

NAIL PUNCH

CHUCK KEY

WOOD GLUE

HAMMER

1 Arrange the mouldings in the finished format of the frame. Position the Stanley clamp so that the corners fit the corners of the frame, with the tightening device at the upper right-hand side on the long side (if you are right-handed). Pull it tight.

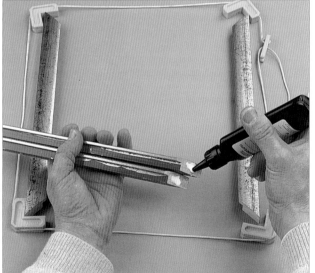

2 Glue the ends of the mouldings together using the wood glue. Squeeze a small amount onto each cut end but take care not to squeeze out too much glue. (If necessary, you can squeeze a blob onto a sheet of card and use a Q-tip to apply it.)

Checklist

Mouldings

Stanley clamp

Wood glue

Drill

Small nails or panel pins

Pliers

Hammer

Nail punch

Plastic wood filler

V-nails (optional)

TIP *In step 3, pull the cord into the V of the locking device sufficiently tightly so that it 'sings' if twanged with the finger after tightening. Wind the cord around the locking device to secure it.*

3 Reposition the mouldings and tighten the clamp with the locking device. Remove any surplus glue that oozes out at the corners. Check the mitres fit, pushing down on them if necessary. Turn over the frame to check the mitres on the reverse side.

4 To prevent the wooden frame from splitting, drill receiving holes for the nails in the frame. To ensure these are the right size, cut the heads off one of the nails with the pliers to make an appropriate sized drill bit. Insert into the chuck of the drill, sharp end outermost, and tighten the drill chuck.

5 Hammer the nails into the drill holes and then punch them in further using the nail punch so that the heads are just below the surface. Cover the holes with plastic wood filler.

USING V-NAILS

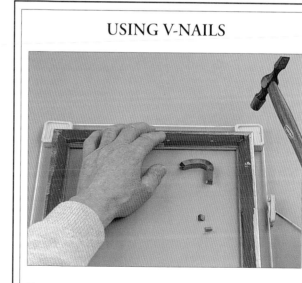

You can join the frame with V-nails, hammering them in from the underside while it is in the clamp. Insert the V-nails on either side of the mitre join.

Cutting Glass

Glass for picture framing is normally bought in large sheets, which you then cut to size using a glass-cutting tool. Since glass breaks easily and the edges are extremely sharp and dangerous, it is important to organize your glass cutting sensibly and carefully. Keep an area of your workroom set aside for glass cutting, if possible, and cover the bench where you cut the glass with a relatively soft but non-hairy material: foam-backed carpet would be ideal.

Roll the protective cover over the sharp edge of the worktop to provide a cushion and to prevent any accidental breakages when you are manoeuvring the glass in sheet form into position before cutting.

Keep a large bin, for any broken glass, close to the glass-cutting area. A hand-held small vacuum cleaner is ideal for clearing up any small shards of glass after glass cutting.

STORING GLASS

Keep the glass stacked vertically in an appropriate rack, which you could make yourself. You will find it easier to retrieve if the glass leans at an angle slightly off the upright (which you can achieve by padding the base of the rack) and if you interleave it with brown paper.

GLASS TYPES

Glass comes in various thicknesses and types, but normally for picture framing you will need to use standard thickness sheet glass (roughly 2mm/¹⁄₁₆in). For some kind of work, you may find that non-reflective glass is best, but it is more expensive than standard glass. Non-reflective glass is particularly useful if you are hanging pictures where the light is coming from behind the viewer.

There are various grades of non-reflective glass, the cheapest tending to grain the image slightly and the most expensive being conservation-quality glass. This helps cut out ultraviolet light, which would otherwise fade the image in time, and causes minimum distortion of the image.

CLEANING GLASS

It is important that the glass is clean, and there is a wide range of proprietary glass cleaners on the market, which will work satisfactorily provided you ensure that you use a clean cloth. Always give the glass a final clean after it is assembled in the frame.

Checklist

Sheet glass

Frame

Straightedge

Glass cutter

Jar with oily rag

Glass cleaner

Lint-free cloth

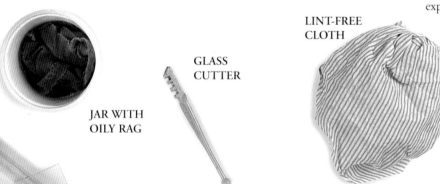

LINT-FREE CLOTH

GLASS CUTTER

JAR WITH OILY RAG

FRAME

SHEET GLASS

STRAIGHTEDGE

GLASS CLEANER

HANDLING GLASS

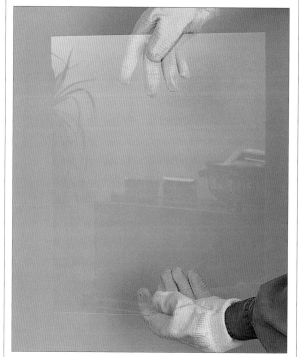

When handling glass, it pays to wear protective glass gloves. Also, you should always handle large sheets of glass vertically, not horizontally, to prevent the glass accidentally snapping as it bows in the centre.

SWIVEL-HEADED
CUTTER

BASIC
CUTTER

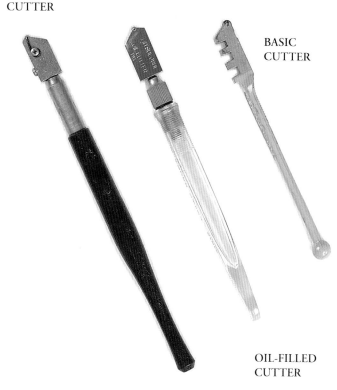

OIL-FILLED
CUTTER

TIP *The basic cutter on the right of the picture to the left is cheaper to purchase and is useful for the beginner as it has notches that nibble bits of glass. The centre cutter is oil-filled, and the cutter on the left has a swivel head which makes it easier to use for cutting curved lines.*

CUTTING GLASS

You will need a certain amount of confidence to cut glass satisfactorily, as well as the appropriate tools for the job. In fact, glass-cutting tools are not expensive, and provided you maintain them carefully, even the simplest kinds will perform well.

Glass-cutting tools should be stored in a jar with a rag soaked in white spirit and oil which will help to keep them lubricated. They should only be lightly moistened, not so wet that the oil from the tool smears the new glass.

When cutting glass, the most important element is the angle of the cutter to the glass. If you do not get this right, you will be unable to cut the glass satisfactorily.

The blade on the glass cutter is angled, and it is to this angle that you need to hold the blade when cutting and ensure that the same angle is used throughout. You must also keep the same pressure from beginning to end of the cut, and keep up the pressure beyond the edge of the glass.

Try out your glass-cutting skills on spare (but not old) pieces of glass before cutting the glass for a frame.

The instructions on the following pages are for cutting sheets of glass up to 60 x 50mm (24 x 20in). If you need a larger sheet, get it cut to measure by a glazier.

CUTTING GLASS

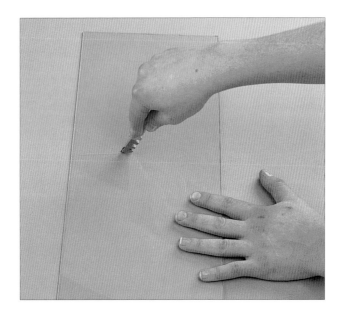

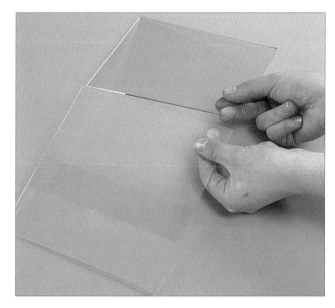

1 Hold the tool at the top end of the handle with the metal part lifted slightly off the glass so that the wheel runs free. To make a lightly scored line, press down on the cutter as you roll it along the glass surface. Continue until the wheel runs off the edge.

2 With thumbs on the top surface of the glass and your forefingers underneath, push upwards close to either side of the scored line. The glass will break along the length of the line.

CUTTING THE GLASS
FOR THE FRAME

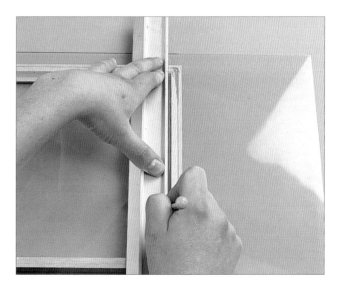

1 Lay the glass on top of the frame, supported by it at each end, so that it is just 1mm/¹⁄₂₄in in from the inner frame edge at one side.

2 On the opposite side, lay the straightedge on the glass lining up the cutter so that the wheel is about 1mm/¹⁄₂₄in in from the end of the frame. Cut the glass against the straightedge, as shown in step 1.

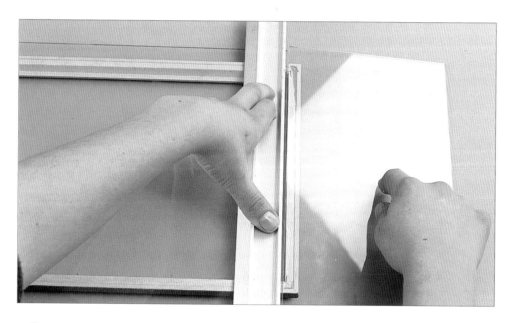

3 Press on the surplus glass, in the centre; it will then snap cleanly down the scored line.

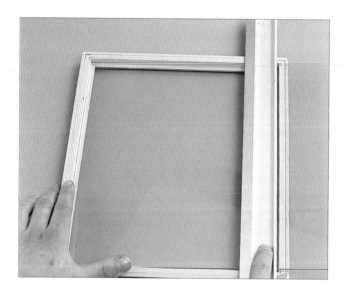

4 Then fit the three sides of the cut glass into the frame and repeat the procedure with the fourth side of the glass (1mm/⅛in from the inner edge of the frame), scoring as in step 2.

5 Break the glass by pulling it slightly towards you off the frame and then pressing with your thumbs on either side of the scored line.

Assembling a Frame

The order in which you assemble the frame depends on whether you are framing one image or several. If you have several to frame, follow the suggestion below right, as it will speed up the process.

Once you have joined the four pieces of mouldings to make the frame and have cut the glass, as well as any mount you intend to use, you can finally assemble the whole frame. You will need a backing board for the picture, of which there are several different forms to choose from. The most popular board is hardboard or medium density fibreboard (MDF), which is normally 2mm/¹⁄₁₆in thick and can be cut relatively easily with a craft knife or a guillotine. Other possible backing boards are corrugated board or foam core board. The latter is expensive but is suitably rigid and very lightweight.

When you are cutting a hardboard backing board, the best system is to measure it off and mark the measurements with a pencil line. Then score down the measured lines with a Stanley knife, but not right through the board. Then break the board down the scoreline.

When positioning the D-rings on the backing board, remember that they normally need to be about one third of the way down from the top of the frame and one quarter of the way in from the sides. Alternatively, position the D-rings sufficiently far apart so that they are behind the mount board and not the image.

Before inserting the glass, remember to clean it thoroughly. Using a piece of cloth, spray glass cleaner onto the cloth and wipe it off. Clean it inside the frame to save cutting your hands.

A useful tool for assembling frames is a Framemaster, (a glazing gun) which drives small wedges called driver points into the frame to keep the backing board in place. Use enough driver points to hold the contents of the frame securely.

ALTERNATIVE

If you wish, you can assemble the frame in the Stanley clamp before you finally nail the frame together. In this case, glue the mouldings together, tighten the Stanley clamp properly (see page 37) and then assemble all the items as shown on the following pages while it is in the clamp. Once the glue is dry, you can remove the frame from the clamp and nail the corners, also as shown on page 37.

Checklist

Frame

Backing board

Pencil

Straightedge

Craft knife

D-rings

Measuring tape

Bradawl

Split rivets

Hammer

Glass

Lint-free cloth

Framemaster

Gummed paper tape

Damp cloth

Cord

DAMP CLOTH

FRAMEMASTER

FRAME

GLASS

MEASURING TAPE

PENCIL

D-RINGS

HAMMER

BACKING BOARD

CORD

GUMMED PAPER TAPE

BRADAWL

1 To cut the backing board, put it into the picture frame and make a mark with a pencil at the edge of the rebate to indicate the correct measurements so that it fits the frame.

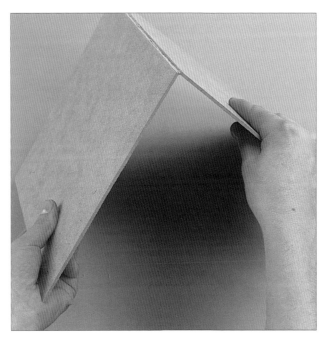

2 Do the same at the base and draw a pencil line to join up the marks. Then score several times down the line with a craft knife against the straightedge. Bend the board so that it breaks down the score line.

3 To position the D-rings on the back put the backing board in the frame and hold the measuring tape against the edge to keep it parallel. Mark off two points each one quarter of the width of the frame in from each side and one third of the depth down from the top.

4 Push the bradawl into the marked holes to punch through the board.

5 Insert a split rivet into the D-rings and push the rivet through the backing board.

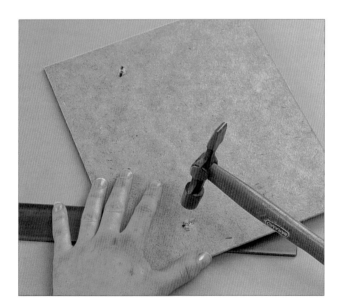

6 Position a piece of metal under the D-ring, open up the split rivets and hammer the rivets back flat.

7 Insert the glass in the frame and clean it thoroughly on both sides.

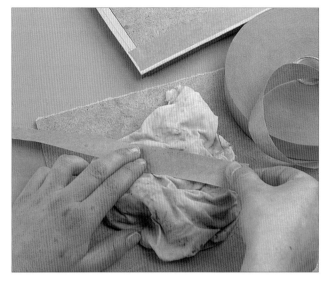

TIP *To transport the picture, fix corrugated cardboard corners to the picture to protect the edges by cutting rectangles of cardboard and then fixing them in position with gummed paper tape.*

8 Put the glass, mount, picture, and backing board into the frame and use the Framemaster to insert the driver points over the backing board. Push the nose into the frame, tilting it slightly and pressing down.

9 Use brown gummed paper tape to cover the join between backing board and frame. Wipe the tape against a damp cloth and then stick it over the backing board and moulding, right around the frame.

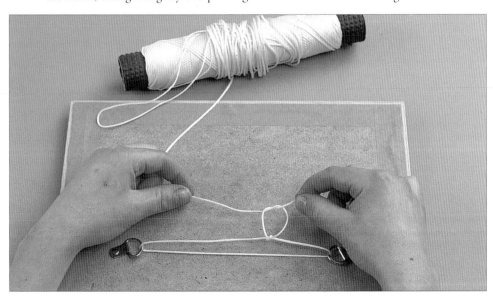

10 Run sufficient picture-hanging cord through the D-rings and then knot the ends three times to secure it in position. (Cord is preferable to wire as it is easier to handle.)

Chapter Two
CUTTING MOUNTS

In this chapter we discuss the ways in which you can cut more elaborate forms of mount than the basic types shown in previous section by using a more sophisticated cutter – the Logan compact cutter. We also show how to cut the basic double mount featured on pages 26-9 using the Logan compact cutter, as this cutter requires a different technique. Cutting mounts accurately and professionally is an important element in picture framing; and with a little practice, the forms shown here are all well within the range of a novice picture framer. More complex mount cutting, such as complete ovals, is not included as this requires even more expensive equipment.

Cutting a Double Mount with a Logan Compact Cutter

While the techniques for cutting a mount using a Logan compact cutter are broadly the same as those for the hand-held cutter, a slightly different approach is needed. The Logan compact cutter has a calibrating bar which enables you to mark off measurements, so you can dispense with border templates. Instead, you can set the cutter to the border widths you require. This makes mount cutting a great deal easier, since you are less likely to make mistakes with the mathematics.

The Logan compact cutter operates in the same way as the hand-held cutter, but the straightedge and body with cutting blade are joined in one unit so there is less risk of the cutter slipping as you make the cut.

With a Logan compact cutter, you cut from the back of the mount card which enables you to work out your measurements on the back of the card, and keeps the top side of the mount card free from fingerprints or dirty marks.

When cutting a single thickness of card on the Logan compact cutter, you will need to insert a second sheet of card underneath to help support the blade and avoid making a ragged cut. If you are cutting a double mount, when two thicknesses of card are inserted in the cutter at the same time, this will not be necessary.

The method described here is for cutting a double mount. In this, the two mounts are placed one on top of each other, the top mount face down beneath the under mount. The aperture is cut through first the under mount and then the top mount. Measure and cut the mount cards to the overall dimensions required for the image (see page 28), remembering to cut the under mount 10mm/⅜in smaller than the top. You could, if you wished, create a triple mount in the same way as this double mount but remember always to measure from the innermost under mount to the outside of the border for the widest measurement, subtracting 5mm/³⁄₁₆in each time, for each under mount.

The Logan compact cutter (above) has a baseboard, setting device, cutter bar and cutting head. The head is removable and can be used as a hand-held cutter if required. Normally, though, it slots into a guiding line on the machine to keep the cutting head and cutter bar united. This ensures that the blade does not slip off the cutting line.

Checklist

Mount cards

Craft knife

Pencil

Logan compact cutter

Double-sided tape or masking tape

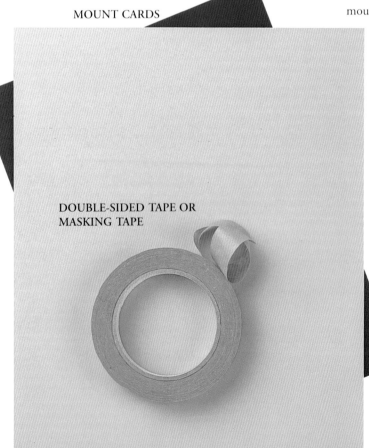

MOUNT CARDS

DOUBLE-SIDED TAPE OR
MASKING TAPE

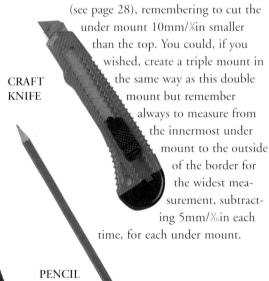

CRAFT
KNIFE

PENCIL

1 Place the top mount face down, and the under mount face down on top. Make a pencil line on both cards on one side to act as a guide, so that you can reposition the cards with the same sides together.

2 Piggy-back the under mount on top of the top mount, face down, and tape them together on all four sides with masking tape.

TIP *First cut the under mount aperture – this border will be the widest measurement, with the top mount border 5mm/³⁄₁₆in narrower. Set the measuring guide on the cutter to the required width (80mm/3³⁄₁₆in here). Insert the under mount, and mark the aperture on the back in pencil, turning the cards in the cutter.*

3 Now insert the mounts in the cutter and mark the aperture as shown in step 3 on page 28. Position the cutter so that the guide mark on the body of the cutter lines up with base line of the aperture.

4 Then use the cutter to cut the aperture as described for cutting a single mount on page 25. When you reach the horizontal cutting line, remember to stop the cutter when the guide mark on the body lines up with the horizontal line. Repeat on the other three sides.

5 Remove the under mount and place the top mount face down, with a cutting card beneath it, in the cutting machine. Reset the bar to the narrower border measurement (75mm/3in in this case) and then cut as before.

6 To ensure the mounts are accurately placed, hinge them first with a small piece of tape and then tape right around to hold them together.

REMOVING THE APERTURE

If one of the corners fails to drop out, insert a razor blade into the cut mark on the coloured side of the mount. Put pressure on the aperture area of the card and slowly let the blade find the correct angle. Draw the blade towards you so that the blade is resting on the bevel. Then gently take the blade up to the corner to release the aperture.

This photograph of a bowl of quinces has been double-mounted using a neutral top mount with a narrow contrasting black border as an under mount.

Cutting a V-groove

A V-groove is a decorative cut line in a mount normally used as an outline for the central image. For it, you need a mount card in which the core is in a contrasting colour to the top layer – either in the form of dark coloured card, or coloured core board. When you cut a V through the top layer, you will reveal this contrasting colour, making a decorative line on the mount card.

To cut a V-groove, you have to cut twice through the core board, each cut forming one side of the V. The first cut is made on the front of the board and the other on the back.

You need a Logan compact cutter for the V-groove because it is impossible to position the cuts accurately enough using a hand-held cutter.

There is a wide range of colours to choose from in core boards. Your selection will depend on the image you are framing, but you can pick either strongly contrasting colours – white with a black core, for example – or much softer, toning colours, such as white with a buff inner core, depending on the style and form of the image.

POSITIONING THE V-GROOVE

The major aesthetic question is where to position the V-groove in relation to the image. You can put the line either fairly close to it, which serves to enclose and emphasize the central image, or leave a wider space between the V-groove and the image, which creates a more decorative effect. Normally, a distance of about 10mm/⅜in works well. You can, if you wish, create two V-grooves – an inner and outer line – but while still learning, it is best to limit yourself to a single V-groove. There is then less opportunity for error.

If you have difficulty in cutting V-grooves successfully, or do not possess a Logan compact cutter, you can create a similar effect simply by decorating the mount with a black ruled line (see page 73).

A 1930s' postcard (taken from a poster for Pears' soap) has been given greater definition with a V-groove cut into a white board with a black central core.

Checklist

Mount card

Pencil or chinagraph pencil

Straightedge

Measuring tape

Logan compact cutter

Sticky tape

Craft knife

Putty rubber

Gummed paper tape

CRAFT
KNIFE

PEN

MOUNT CARD

TIP *When cutting a V-groove, one cut is made on the front of the board (just as if cutting a single mount – see page 25) and the second is made 1mm/¹⁄₂₄in nearer to the border on the reverse of the board.*

1 Cut the card to the overall measurements required (see pages 22-3). Then estimate the proportions of the border and the V-groove and mark their positions in pencil or with a chinagraph pencil on the back of the mount. Mark the aperture with a straight line, and the V-groove with a wiggly line to distinguish between them.

2 Having decided on the proportions, measure the width of the border and the width of the V-groove using the measuring tape, eg the V-groove lies 60mm/2⅜in in from the outer edge of the mount, and the border is 70mm/2¾in wide. Note down these measurements on a spare piece of card.

3 Insert the mount card face up in the cutter, with a cutting card beneath. Set the calibrating bar to the measurement required for the first cut of the V-groove (here, 60mm/2⅜in). Very lightly pencil in the cutting lines on the card.

4 Position the cutter to cut the first line of the V-groove, lining up the guide mark on the body of the cutter with the base cutting line of the V-groove. Begin to cut the V-groove, cutting up and away from you. When cutting, use your free hand to hold and control the cutter. You need to place downward pressure on the cutter to stop it sliding about.

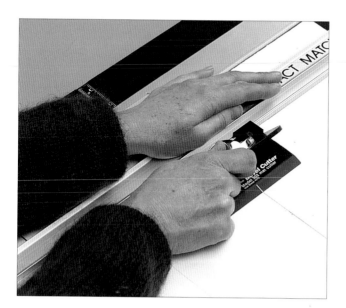

5 Make sure that you end each V-groove cut with the guide mark on the body of the cutter on the pencil marked line you are moving towards.

6 To hold the mount together, tape it up on the reverse side as you cut through each side of the V-groove, reinserting the card each time, face up.

TIP *The positioning for the second line of the V-groove must be absolutely accurate otherwise you will not create a clean-cut line. Remember that you cut the first V-groove on the top surface of the mount and the second on the under surface.*

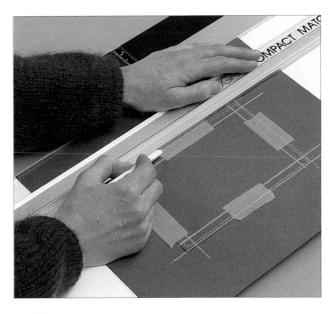

7 On the reverse side now, make the other cut for the V-groove. Move the calibrating bar in by 1mm/⅛in Place the mount card back in the cutter, but face down now, and draw the other lines of the V-groove.

8 Make the second cut for the V-groove, as before, turning the card clockwise each time until all four sides are cut.

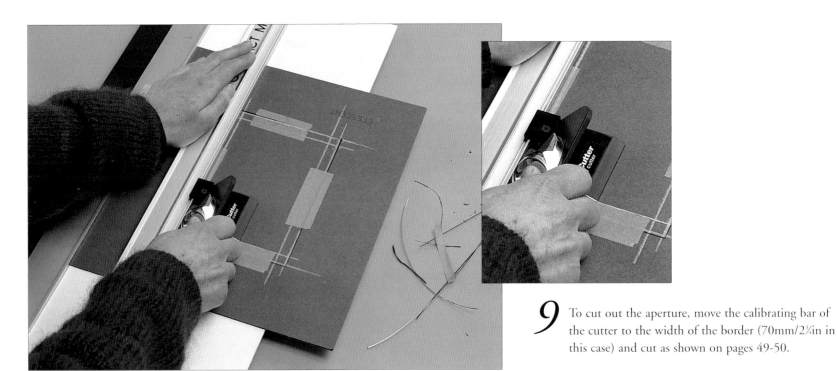

9 To cut out the aperture, move the calibrating bar of the cutter to the width of the border (70mm/2⅜in in this case) and cut as shown on pages 49-50.

10 After the aperture has dropped out rub out the pencil lines you made to mark the V-groove, using a putty rubber.

11 To ensure that the mount is positioned correctly over the image, place a piece of tape on the bottom of the image. Once the image is correctly positioned, press down on the tape.

12 To keep the image firmly in place, tape around the back of the image using the gummed paper tape.

Cutting a Triple Aperture Mount with a V-groove

If you have a range of differently-sized images, you can, of course, create appropriate-sized apertures for them in a single sheet of mount card. Try to organize them in an aesthetically pleasing way, perhaps with two smaller images on each side of a larger one.

You may well, at some point, wish to frame more than one small image within the same piece of mount card, either with a double aperture or a triple one, as here. The items shown here, old German banknotes, look good positioned vertically, but you may well decide to create a multiple aperture mount that runs horizontally instead. Whichever you decide to do, the principle is the same – you have to carefully work out the measurements of the borders and the areas between the apertures to ensure that you make the cuts for them where required.

Cutting two or more apertures in a single piece of card is clearly more taxing that cutting one, since you increase the likelihood of error. So it is important to keep a clear head when working out the mathematics for the positioning of the apertures. Check and double-check these before you cut.

For these banknotes, which are fairly small, it was decided to embellish the mount with a V-groove to help unite and emphasize them in the mount. A simple V-groove or line provides a useful linking device for this kind of mount.

To determine the width of the space in between the pictures, use the general principle that it should be half the width of your outer border.

The three bank notes have been positioned vertically, one above the other in a toning, neutral coloured card with a black core. The V-groove is a framing and linking device just outside the three images.

Checklist

Dark-coloured mount card or core board

Measuring tape

Pencil

Chinagraph pencil

Eraser

Logan compact cutter

Razor blade

Craft knife

Backing board (acid-free)

Acid-free tape

BACKING BOARD (ACID-FREE)

MOUNT CARD

MEASURING TAPE

PENCIL

CHINAGRAPH PENCIL

ERASER

CRAFT KNIFE

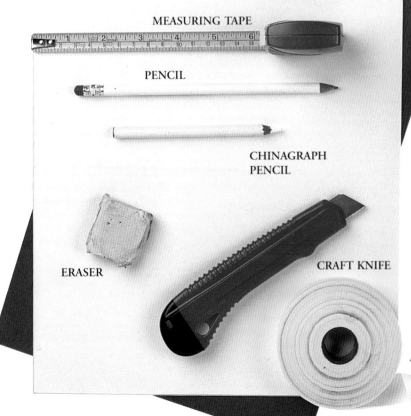

ACID-FREE TAPE

TIP *Cross-check your measurements by marking them down both sides of the board. If they are accurate, you will be able to join them up neatly across the width of the apertures.*

1   First choose an appropriate coloured mount card or, as here, core board to complement all three images. Work out the desired border widths for the images by trying out templates or corner pieces of mount card.

2   Measure the depth of the images, and mark these in order from the top of the mount down. Then add the depths of the images to the depths of the desired borders, surrounding and in between the images. This will give you the overall vertical measurement of the mount card. Do the same with the widths of the images and borders to determine the horizontal measurement of the card.

3 Cut the board to the overall measurements (see page 23.) Then plot the positions of the images on the back of the mount card, marking off the measurements and positioning the images as a double check.

4 Mark the position of the V-groove (see page 54) and then cut it, remembering to cut on both sides of the mount (as on pages 55-6).

TIPS *On the back of the mount card in step 3, denote the spaces between the pictures with a squiggly line to make sure you do not slice through them.*
When cutting through the apertures in step 4, start from the base, cutting away from you, and always turn the mount clockwise.

5 Now cut the apertures. To make sure that the angle of the bevel is correct (sloping out from the centre to the outer edge), it is important to cut particular the outer edges of the aperture first, and then the inner, pushing the cutter away from you.

6 If any of the apertures don't fall out neatly, gently cut the corners of the aperture with a razor blade to remove them more accurately – as described in the tip on page 50.

7 Carefully remove any excess tape from the back with a craft knife so that it doesn't show on the front.

8 Cut a piece of acid-free backing board to the same size as the mount by placing the mount on top, lining up the edges and then cutting around it. Hold the mount firmly so that it doesn't slide about.

9 Hinge the top of the mount to the backing board and then use small, hinge-like pieces of tape to position the pictures one by one on the backing board. When working with several images in a triple mount, it is important that you position them accurately in the apertures you have cut.

Cutting an Arched Mount

Normally, mounts with any kind of circular aperture are cut on a special oval cutter, which a novice picture framer may not have access to. However, by using both a hand-held Cushway cutter and a Logan compact cutter, a compromise can be reached. The result is a semi-circular arch to the mount, with a small shoulder step on either side. The reason for including the shoulder steps is that they enable you to join the curved part of the aperture to the straight elements without unattractive join marks.

Arched mounts are particularly successful for framing an image where the top of the picture fades away. In this case, it has been used for an old sepia family photograph and focuses attention on the subject, eliminating the background.

To decide how deep to make the arch, and where to position the shoulders, you first need to establish the diameter of the image, the size of the aperture and also the size of the finished mount.

Checklist

Measuring tape

Pencil

Mount card

Compass

Straightedge

Logan compact cutter

Cushway cutter

Eraser

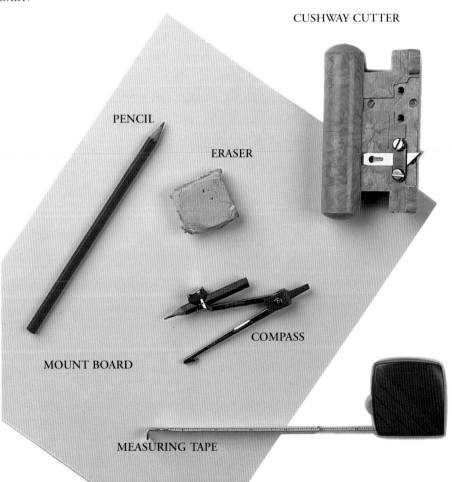

CUSHWAY CUTTER

PENCIL

ERASER

COMPASS

MOUNT BOARD

MEASURING TAPE

1 First measure the image so that you can decide on the overall dimensions of the mount card.

2 Then work out the overall area of the aperture from the top of the arch to the base, and the width. Mark this on the back of the mount card.

Opposite: The sepia family photograph, with its poorly defined background, was given definition with this arched mount. The buff-coloured mount card and natural wood frame help to keep the period feel of the image.

4 With a piece of cutting board beneath the mount card (face down), use the Cushway cutter to cut out the arch. Put the blade on the line and push it along to cut around the arch. It does not matter if you cut into the aperture as this will be cut away eventually.

3 Measure the shoulder points of the arch on the aperture and the central point of the arch on the horizontal top line. With a compass fixed on this central mark, measure a semi-circle below it to the width of the aperture less 10mm/⅜in. At the centre of the semicircle, draw a second circle to the same width – this forms the arch.

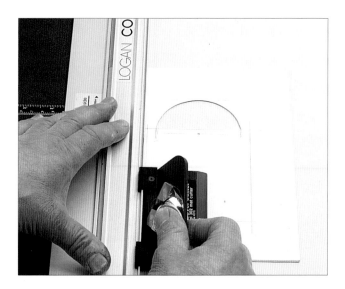

5 Cut the shoulders with the Logan cutter set to the appropriate width (here it is 75mm/3in). Then cut the remaining borders with the cutter positioned to your noted measurement (here it is 40mm/1½in).

Chapter Three
DECORATING MOUNTS

This chapter looks at some of the ways in which you can decorate mounts, including marbled strip lines, various forms of wash line and stencilled and stamped designs.

The aim of these decorations is to enhance the central image in some way, so it is important to remember that it is the image that is the focus, and the mount decoration merely an accessory. Subtlety and sensitivity are therefore key elements of such decoration; beware of creating such a strong effect with the mount decoration that it dominates the image.

Using Marbled Paper Strips and Ruled Lines

For this relatively delicate image in sepia and soft blue on a cream paper, a cream mount that matches the colour of the photographic paper was chosen to make the subject the most dominant element. A marbled paper, cut to a 3mm/⅛in width, was used as the main decoration, and a thinner, 2mm/¹⁄₁₆in-wide ruled line in a shade of blue that matches the child's coat, was used for the inner line (see page 73). A gold line, spaced slightly further away from the marbled paper was then used for the outer line.

Marbled paper has a long tradition in all kinds of papercraft and was used traditionally in book binding, either for end-papers or as cover papers, with neatly worked leather corners.

You can, if you choose, create your own marbled papers very simply in a bath of oil-based pigments floating in water. The paper is dragged by hand, or by machine, through the bath, creating the familiar swirling patterns that resemble the grain of marble. Some of the very best marbled papers are hand-made in Italy.

Although the design here uses marble strips, you could cover the whole mount in marbled paper, possibly as a decoration for a certificate or similar image. All you need to do is apply the marbled paper to the mount card using PVA glue and then cut out the mount aperture in the normal way.

Be careful not to waste expensive marbled paper; keep unused paper neatly rolled or, if provided with its own backing board, in a plastic cover.

Checklist

Mount card

Marbled paper

Corner marking gauge

Pencil or needle

Non-slip straightedge with bevelled edge

Multi-cutter

Craft knife

Watercolours (ultramarine, cobalt, viridian)

Palette

Paintbrushes

Ruling pen

Gold ink

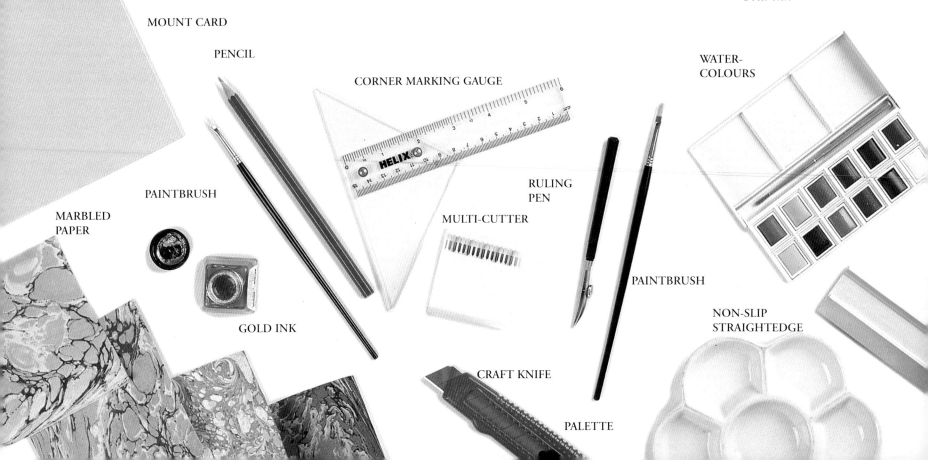

MOUNT CARD

PENCIL

CORNER MARKING GAUGE

WATER-COLOURS

PAINTBRUSH

RULING PEN

MARBLED PAPER

MULTI-CUTTER

PAINTBRUSH

GOLD INK

NON-SLIP STRAIGHTEDGE

CRAFT KNIFE

PALETTE

The mount for this hand-tinted photograph has been decorated with toning marble strip lines, surrounded by blue and gold ruled lines. The instructions for marble strip lines follow, and those for the ruled lines are to be found on page 73.

MARBLED PAPERS

A selection of marbled papers demonstrates their wonderfully subtle patterning. Most good art supply shops have a range to choose from or they can be obtained in a wider variety from specialist fine paper suppliers.

Marbled paper strips are a relatively simple form of decoration. You can use them on their own or with ruled lines, as shown in this project. For this particular image, the decoration consists of a marbled paper line (see below and overleaf) and a blue and gold ruled line on either side (see page 73). The width chosen for the marbled paper lines in this case was relatively narrow (3mm/⅛in), but you can make them wider if you feel the subject would benefit.

To create fine lines using marbled paper, you will need a multi-cutter – a tool that cuts the paper into even strips as narrow as 3mm/⅛in. You can adjust the blades of the multi-cutter to the required width and it will cut all four strips for the mount simultaneously.

If you buy the marbled paper already fixed to a self-adhesive backing, you can simply peel the strips off the backing as you need them. Otherwise, you will need to back the marbled paper with double-sided tape before cutting the strips. These ready-mounted marbled papers can be bought from specialist suppliers, as can the multi-cutter (see page 141). To mark out the positions of the lines, you can use either a sharp, long needle or a pencil with a fine lead.

MARBLED PAPER
STRIPS

1 After preparing the mount and cutting out the aperture (see pages 22-5), decide on the position of the strips of marbled paper and the ruled lines. The strips should be positioned before the ruled lines. Using the corner marking gauge and a long, sharp needle or a pencil, mark the distance from the aperture, at each corner, where the first strip will be positioned.

2 Using a sharp pencil and straightedge, connect the four corners by drawing fine pencil lines. These will not show when the decoration is complete. Don't be tempted to skip this step, as the strip of marbled paper will bow, and you will need a guideline to keep it straight.

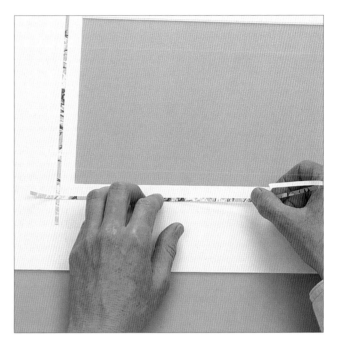

3 Insert five blades into the multi-cutter, placing them the required distance apart – 3mm/⅛in in this case – to cut four strips. Using the straightedge to guide the cutter, cut the four strips so that they are slightly longer than required. You will need to use quite a lot of pressure. When you have finished cutting, replace the cover for safety.

4 Peel the backing off the first strip and then position it along one of the pencil lines. Once the strip is straight, press it down, working from left to right. Repeat for the other three strips. The ends should overlap at the corners, but do not press down at the corners yet.

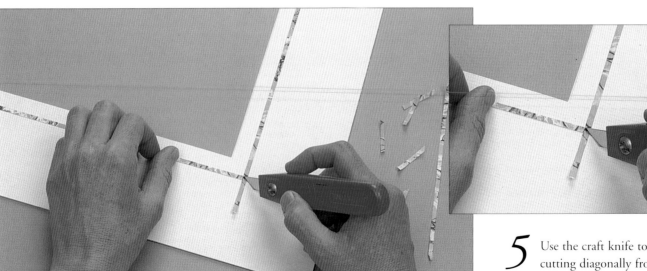

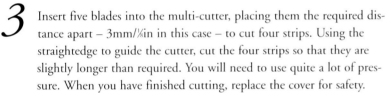

5 Use the craft knife to cut a neat mitre at each corner, cutting diagonally from the inside of the corner to the outside. Press down, removing the surplus strip.

MAKING RULED LINES

Make more than enough diluted wash to draw the required lines. To charge the ruling pen, dip a paintbrush into the medium and then stroke the brush across the bowed side of the pen, with the flat side downwards. If you do get some of the medium on the front of the pen, wipe it off before you start. Ideally, charge the pen with enough of the medium to complete one full line at a time. Draw a short practice line first to get the pen flowing.

1 To create the ruled wash line, mix up a diluted wash in your palette and try out the effect on some scrap board. Then use the corner marking gauge to mark out the corner points of the ruled lines in the same way as you did the strips of marbled paper on page 71, but this time do not join up the marks.

2 Place the straightedge so that the two corner marks at the bottom of the mount line up. Then, charge the ruling pen as described (right) and with the flat side of the pen next to the straightedge and keeping it vertical, draw the first line. Repeat with the other three lines.

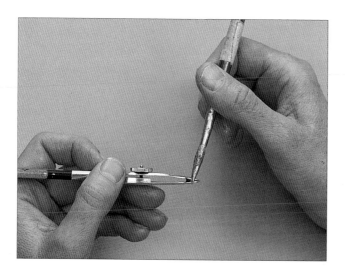

3 To create the gold line, using a different ruling pen, paintbrush and part of the palette for the gold ink, charge the ruling pen as before. If the gold ink does not run smoothly, dilute it with a little water.

4 Use the ruling pen to draw the first gold line, just as in step 2. Then clean out the sediments from the reservoir of the ruling pen, and recharge it, as before. Draw the three remaining lines in the same way.

Making a Line and Wash

Once you have mastered decorating the mount with a simple ruled line you can try your hand at line and wash, which consists of a narrow panel of washed colour between two lines. The central area of washed colour is normally executed in a diluted wash, picking up one of the colours from the image itself.

This kind of decoration is particularly useful for classic images such as botanical prints, for example, or for simple landscapes in subtle watercolours. If you are using coloured washes, aim to pick up one of the colours in the central image to successfully tie-in the mount.

The surrounding lines could be executed in slightly deeper tones or even in gold ink. You can have just two lines, containing the wash, or more as you wish. When spacing the lines, take care to ensure that they do not dominate the mount. This kind of decoration often looks best if contained within the inner third of the mount border.

PRACTICAL ELEMENTS

When you are working with a limited edition print, or any similarly valuable image, it pays to use all acid-free materials, including the mount board and the tape and base board on which they are mounted. Acid-free board helps to prolong the life of a picture and it also helps to prevent foxing – little brown spots that mottle the mount, caused by dampness and condensation.

When working with watercolour washes, load the brush fairly well, make a small puddle of colour on the card, and then draw this out within the ruled lines, as shown opposite and overleaf. It is important to ensure there is no waterline at the corner of the border where the most recent brush marks join the first ones. To avoid this, wet a small square at the corner using plain water, before you start.

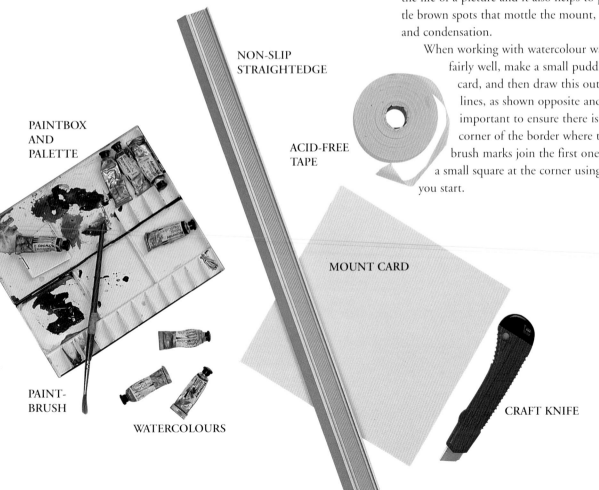

PAINTBOX AND PALETTE

NON-SLIP STRAIGHTEDGE

ACID-FREE TAPE

MOUNT CARD

PAINT-BRUSH

WATERCOLOURS

CRAFT KNIFE

Checklist

Mount card

Corner marking gauge

Pencil

Paintbrush

Ruling pen

Non-slip straightedge

Watercolours

Palette

Acid-free tape

Craft knife

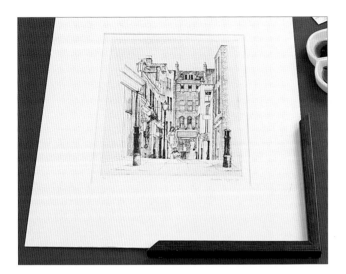

1 Choose the style of the decoration, the colour and size of the mount and the colour of the ruled and wash lines, usually tones chosen from the original image. Cut out the mount, making it slightly larger than usual.

2 Working from the aperture outwards, use the corner marking gauge to measure the position of the line nearest to the aperture. Mark the corner point with a pencil or needle. Repeat at each corner and then repeat for the outer lines that will contain the wash.

3 Rule the lines as shown on page 73, having first tested the colours on a spare piece of mount card. Always keep the pen at right angles to the straightedge and rule the lines, working from the inner line outwards. Let the lines dry before adding the wash.

4 The brush for the wash must be spotless before you start. Put a dab of clear water in the first corner between the ruled lines and brush a little square. Then stir the colour well, dip the brush in and make a diagonal stroke in this square to start the wash.

5 Make a puddle of colour and draw it along the mount with the brush. Before the puddle disappears, stir the paint, recharge the brush and continue as before. Stir the paint between each application.

6 When you have worked around the mount clockwise almost to the point where you started, draw the last puddle of paint out until it meets the diagonal at the start. This will prevent any watermark.

7 Allow the wash to dry, rule any remaining lines and then hinge the image to the mount card.

8 Position the mount carefully onto the image, pressing it in place once it is correctly positioned.

The finished wash and ruled line decoration, with its subtle toning colours, provides an attractive frame for the central image.

Potato Stamping

Simple and very attractive designs can be made on a mount by stamping a repeating pattern on to it, using either a ready-made bought stamp, or one you have cut yourself. For simple designs, a potato makes a suitable stamping tool. You will find that you can make only a fairly limited range of basic shapes such as small diamonds, stars or the hearts used here, but they are nonetheless very effective. Here a double-stamped effect was created by overprinting the design in a different colour.

A variety of paints can be used for stamping, but a water-based acrylic paint is the easiest to use. The paint must not be too runny or the image will not stamp with a crisp edge. Always test the stamp, and the paint, first on a piece of test card – ideally of the same kind and colour as the one chosen for the finished mount.

The hearts chosen here echo the central image of the picture and were stamped first in red, and then over-stamped in gold, after reducing the dimensions of the stamp to prevent the second colour from spreading out over the first.

Checklist

Large potato

Scalpel

Permanent marker pen

Image to be copied

Craft knife

Mounting card

Acrylic paints

Palette

Paintbrush

Double-sided tape

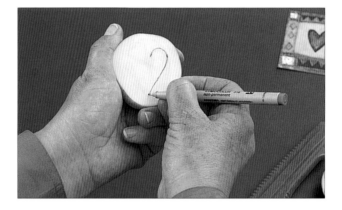

1 Take a suitably sized potato, ideally with waxy flesh. (If the potato is wet, let it dry after cutting.) Having cut it in half, draw the chosen image on the potato using the permanent marker pen.

MOUNT CARD

PERMANENT MARKER PEN

DOUBLE-SIDED TAPE

PAINTBRUSH

LARGE POTATO

SCALPEL

CRAFT KNIFE

ACRYLIC PAINTS

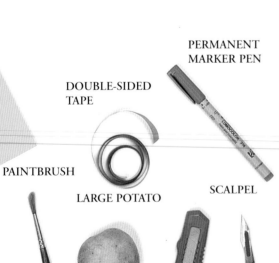

2 Using the craft knife, cut around the marked image on the potato, taking care not to cut through the line or to cut your fingers as you do so!

Note how the background colour of the finished stamped mount harmonizes with the background of the central image, while the stamped decoration matches the colour of the central heart motif.

TIP *If you want to position the stamped images precisely, you will need to mark the mount accordingly, using a fine pencil guide mark on the mount. In this case, a freehand approach was chosen, and the hearts stamped by eye, creating an attractive random effect.*

3 Mix up the chosen paint colour, and brush the paint onto the raised area of the stamp. Practise stamping the image on similar coloured card until you are satisfied that it is printing properly, and the appropriate amount of paint for doing so can be verified.

4 To achieve the decorations used here, stamp the four corners of the mount with the heart stamp, working from top to bottom and left to right of the mount to avoid smudging the final effect. Allow the paint to dry before continuing.

5 To over-stamp the hearts using a paler orange-yellow paint, cut the heart stamp down in size slightly, and then overprint to give a yellowish centre.

6 To finish, back the under mount onto the mounting board. Then tape the back of the central image along the two vertical sides with double-sided tape, before positioning it in the centre of the aperture.

Stencilling

Stencilling is a centuries-old decorative technique which enables craftsmen to mimic the work of artists by duplicating an already drawn or painted image. This is then cut out to make a stencil and used as a template for painting. Stencils can be used for borders and are extraordinarily versatile as they can be used in a continuous, linked motif, or as a one-off decoration.

For mount decoration, stencilling works well if employed with a fairly simple central image. You can use it as an all-round border, or as a one-off decorative device in a corner of the mount. It is important that the stencil decoration does not overwhelm or dominate the central image, so do not make it larger than the image itself. It also pays to keep the colours toning, and subtle, rather than strong or strident.

You can cut your own stencils quite easily which gives you far greater scope than using ready-bought stencils. Ideally, a transparent film, such as acetate, is used so that you can see what you are doing. A marking pen used to trace off the image can be wiped away if a mistake is made.

It is important that you simplify the image to be sten-cilled so that you can cut it out easily. You also need to leave wide enough bridges of stencil acetate to make it durable. Start by doing simple, larger shapes.

The best colours to use are powder paints used dry, as you can mix the colours together very well, giving a subtle, blended effect, rather like air brushing. But they will need to be sealed afterwards with pastel fixative. Equally, you can use special stencil paints if you prefer.

For larger stencils, use a paintbrush or special stencil brush instead of the Q-tips to apply the paint.

Checklist

Sheet of acetate (or similar)

Permanent marker pen (fine tipped)

Masking tape

Scalpel

Backing board

Powder paints

Q-tips

Pastel fixative

BACKING BOARD

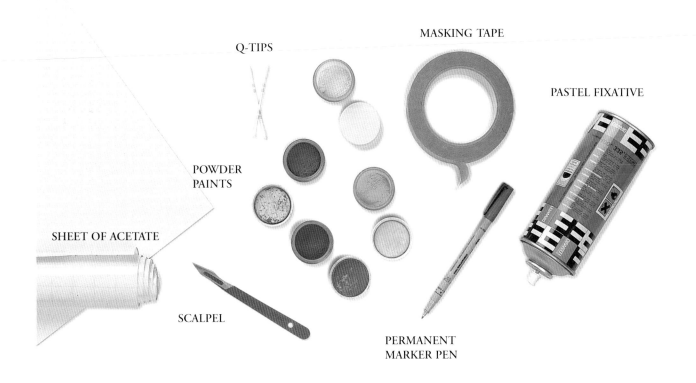

Q-TIPS

MASKING TAPE

PASTEL FIXATIVE

POWDER PAINTS

SHEET OF ACETATE

SCALPEL

PERMANENT MARKER PEN

TIP *You can mix the powder paints on a piece of card to achieve subtle tones and hues. You need a mid-blue, a yellow, a red, and a white. All the other colours can be mixed using these.*

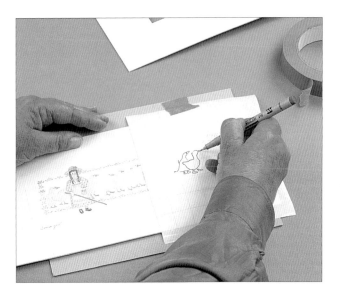

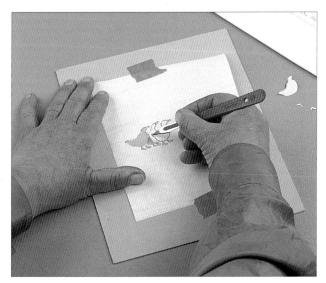

1 Position the sheet of acetate over the image and fasten in place leaving a wide border around the edges. Then trace over the image with the permanent marker pen. Remove the acetate.

2 Cut out the traced images with the scalpel on a backing board to prevent cutting through your work surface. Leave a piece around any cut image to make a bridge so that the whole image does not disappear.

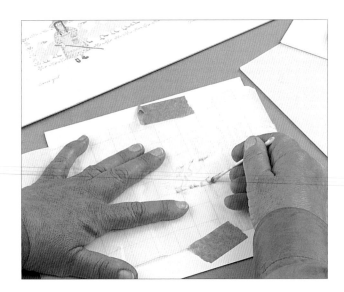

3 Tape the finished stencil to a spare piece of card to test the colours. Use the powder paints and a Q-tip to apply them.

4 Once you are happy with the colours, position the stencil on the mount, fix it lightly in place, and apply the paint. Paint the larger areas first, applying the colours one by one. Keep blowing away the surplus powder. Repeat the design as many or as few times as you like. When the stencil is finished, spray the dry powder with pastel fixative.

This little picture for a child's room has been given the addition of a stencilled design in one corner of the mount. The motif has been taken from the main picture.

Chapter Four
DECORATING FRAMES

The frame to a picture can be very simple – perhaps made from a particularly beautiful wood, for example – or it can be highly decorative. Your choice will depend on the form and style of the subject to be framed, but there are various finishes you can opt for. Some, such as crackle glazing (see pages 86-9) and verdigris (see pages 90-3), are fairly subtle variations to the overall colour and texture of the frame. Others use more decorative devices, such as stamping and stencilling (already covered in Decorating Mounts on pages 78-83), and découpage (see pages 98-101), which make a pictorial object of the frame itself. These need to be used with care when framing images, as they should enhance and not overwhelm the subject.

Crackle Glazing

Highly polished varnished surfaces, known as lacquer work, were extremely popular in the 17th and 18th centuries and involved patient applications of many layers of varnish until a smooth, gleaming finish was created in which no brush mark was to be seen. Occasionally, less well-varnished surfaces broke up in time, creating a maze of tiny hairline cracks in the surface. This finish has come to be seen as attractive in its own right, and can be imitated by cheating!

If you use two varnishes with a different chemical base, they react against each other, and the top coat then splits into hairline cracks. If a little dark wax or paint is rubbed into these, the cracks will be revealed still more, like in an antique painting. Nowadays, you can buy the varnishes required as a kit of crackle varnish.

It is important that you crackle glaze over a non-porous surface, such as one which has been painted and then varnished with acrylic varnish.

The second coat of water-based crackle varnish has to be applied when the first coat of oil-based varnish is still just slightly tacky but not sticky. If you wait until it is too dry, the effect will not 'crackle' properly. The warmer the atmosphere, the quicker the varnish will dry, but normally it will take about an hour. You can speed up the process by using a hair dryer.

Crackle glazing gives an attractive antiqued finish which is ideal when framing old prints and reproductions, for example.

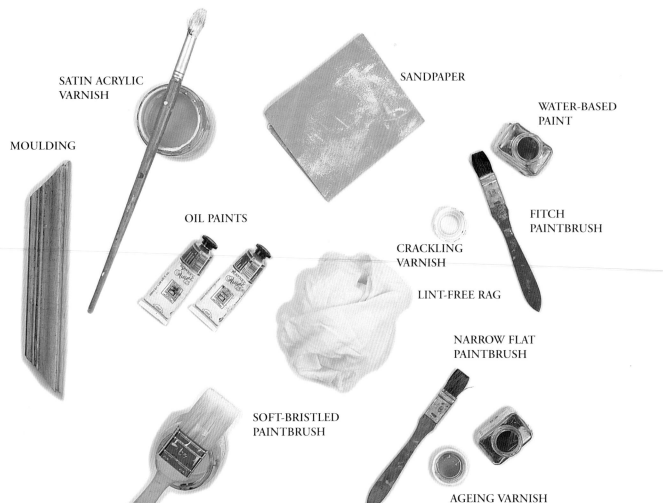

SATIN ACRYLIC
VARNISH

SANDPAPER

WATER-BASED
PAINT

MOULDING

OIL PAINTS

CRACKLING
VARNISH

FITCH
PAINTBRUSH

LINT-FREE RAG

NARROW FLAT
PAINTBRUSH

SOFT-BRISTLED
PAINTBRUSH

AGEING VARNISH

Checklist

Moulding

Sandpaper (coarse grade)

Water-based paint (off-white)

Paintbrushes (fitch, flat soft-bristled)

Satin acrylic varnish

Ageing varnish

Crackling varnish

Oil paints (chromium green, burnt umber, raw umber)

Lint-free rag

One of the most successful ways to achieve an aged look is to use a cream or off-white base coat which will then 'age' into a soft creamy brown once the crackle varnish is applied. Remember that dark wax or pigment must be rubbed into the cracks so that they show up well.

1 Sand the frame with fairly coarse sandpaper to remove any existing varnish.

2 Paint the frame with the off-white water-based paint using the fitch and then repeat with a second coat of the same when the first is dry.

3 When the base coat is dry, varnish with the satin acrylic varnish using the very soft bristled brush. Allow to dry and give it a second coat. This gives a suitably smooth finish for the ageing varnish.

4 Apply a coat of the ageing varnish (which is oil-based) using a narrower soft-bristled brush and leave until it is tacky (but not sticky). This takes about 30 minutes, depending on the temperature of the room.

5 Apply the crackling varnish using the narrower soft-bristled brush. Accelerate the drying (and the consequent cracking) using hot air from a hand-held hair dryer and then leave to dry for a couple of hours.

6 Using your finger, rub some oil paint of a dark colour into the cracks – here a mixture of chromium green, burnt umber and raw umber was used.

7 Rub off any surplus using a lint-free rag. If you accidentally let the paint harden, you can soften it, with care, with a turpentine-soaked rag.

8 Protect the moulding with a coat of oil-based varnish applied with a small paintbrush. Either use the ageing varnish used in step 4, or apply a coat of polyurethane varnish.

Verdigris

Verdigris, the natural patina that marks brass and copper with a greenish-blue mottled bloom, can be recreated deliberately using paints to make a very attractive finish for a frame. The colour and pattern that verdigris produces is never uniform, so feel free to experiment with colours, tones and patterns.

A verdigris effect on a frame works very well with photographs and simple black and white line drawings, for example. You can, if you wish, buy one of the proprietary verdigris paints, but it is not difficult to create it yourself from acrylics, and it is certainly cheaper. You will find it helps to produce a realistic effect if you study a piece of bronze or copper that has acquired a natural verdigris patina such as the antique candlestick featured in the photograph below. It has slowly become covered with a genuine layer of verdigris.

For this frame, a slightly antiqued finish was created, and a small amount of gilding cream provided the finishing touch. The antiquing effect – rubbing back with fine grade wire wool, and then using gilding cream as the last step – could equally be copied on any painted frame. If you paint the base coat a darker colour than the top coat, and then rub back the top coat as shown here, you will get the broken, 'antiqued' look that is currently very fashionable.

Checklist

Acrylic paints (deep grey, Farlow green, cadmium yellow)

Wide artist's paintbrush

Sponge

Wire wool (fine grade)

Gilding cream

Soft cloth

Mount card

MOUNT CARD

WIDE ARTIST'S PAINTBRUSH

SPONGE

GILDING CREAM

ANTIQUE CANDLESTICK WITH GENUINE VERDIGRIS FOR REFERENCE

ACRYLIC GESSO

ACRYLIC PAINTS

WIRE WOOL

1 Mix up some deep battleship grey acrylic paint (either ready-made or made from black paint mixed with white acrylic gesso, which is a thicker than normal paint). Paint the frame and allow to dry.

2 Mix together greenish blue and yellow acrylic paint (Farlow green and cadmium yellow were used here) to create the right verdigris colour.

3 Practise getting the right verdigris colour by dabbing the mixed paint on a sheet of card, using a sponge, until you are satisfied with the shade. Vary the proportions of the colours until you have achieved the desired colour.

Opposite: The verdigris paint effect on this frame enhances the muted shades of the central image and cleverly echoes the worn paintwork on the metal park chairs.

4 Lightly sponge the verdigris colour over the grey base coat, taking care to create a suitably dappled effect. Allow to dry.

5 Using some of the fine grade wire wool, very lightly rub back the verdigris coat in places. This will help to make the verdigris look less evenly painted, and so more natural.

6 Rub in a little gilding cream to the raised parts of the moulding. Allow to dry, then buff up with the soft cloth.

Resist-painting

Frames can be painted either very simply, using a couple of coats of acrylic paint, or you can create a more elaborately decorated painted frame. The methods you use can vary from stencilling and stamping (as executed in Decorating Mounts on pages 66-83) to this particular form of decoration which uses a blocking agent to prevent the second colour adhering to certain parts of the frame, revealing the pattern in the base coat colour.

In the past, this kind of technique was carried out using wax as the resisting medium since paint will not adhere to wax – but modern masking fluid is easier to use and readily available from art supply stores.

If you use acrylic artist's paints, you can mix them with standard white acrylic paint until you get exactly the right shade you want, which is cheaper than buying cans of specially mixed colours. Be warned, however, that a little of the darker acrylic colours go a lot further than you think. Mix up the colours on a small plate, until you work out exactly how many drops of pure acrylic colour you need to create the right shade.

The antiqued effect shown in the last two steps overleaf, is not essential, but it helps to give the frame an attractive patina, and tones down the colour of the paint quite considerably. The darker the finishing wax, the more subdued the overall colour will be. It can be a useful way to correct an over-bright painted frame.

A postcard of a flamboyantly coloured Matisse picture deserves a similarly bold framing treatment. The pattern on the girl's headscarf inspired the design for the frame decoration.

ANTIQUE PINE WAX

SAMPLES OF MOULDINGS WITH RESIST TECHNIQUE DECORATION

WIRE WOOL

MASKING FLUID

SOFT CLOTH

SCALPEL

PAINTBRUSH

WATER-BASED PAINTS

Checklist

Water-based paints (yellow ochre, vermilion, blue-black)

Paintbrushes (fine and medium artist's)

Masking fluid

Scalpel

Wire wool (fine grade)

Antique pine wax

Soft cloth

TIP *When creating a resist-painted design, do not make it too complicated as peeling off the resist medium is quite laborious and time-consuming. On a large frame, keep the design fairly simple.*

1 Paint the frame with the water-based paint, choosing a colour that appears in the image as this colour will eventually show as the design on the frame. In this case, a water-based yellow ochre brightened with yellow pigment was used. Allow to dry.

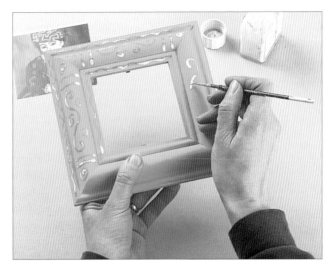

2 Paint the chosen design in masking fluid on the base coat. Make sure the masking fluid is applied thickly enough, and do not attempt fine patterns. The design must be fairly basic. Allow the fluid to dry; it will be transparent when dry.

3 Paint over the whole frame, including the masking fluid design, with a water-based red paint (here, a strong vermilion). Do not apply it too thickly or the masking fluid will fail to peel off later. Allow the paint to dry.

4 Start to peel off the masking fluid, using the scalpel to lift it and then pulling the strips off with your fingers.

TIP *Adding a little darker-coloured paint to the raised edges of the mouldings, together with the finishing wax, helps give the decorated frame a more attractive, subtly aged appearance.*

5 Roughly paint a little blue-black paint onto the raised edges of the mouldings and around the sides of the frame. Allow to dry.

6 Wax the front of the frame all over with some of the fine wire wool and the antique pine wax, rubbing the wax well in.

7 Allow the wax to dry for about 15 minutes and then buff up the frame with a soft cloth. The end result is a sumptuous, gleaming picture frame that richly enhances the image.

Découpage

If you wish to create a fairly elaborately decorated frame, découpage – in which images are cut out and stuck down on the frame – is the ideal solution. It is extremely easy to do, and produces a professional result with relatively little skill.

Popular in Victorian times, when pattern books were employed for the purpose, découpage has recently become very popular once again. For the images, you could either take them (either cut out or photocopied) from modern fac-simile pattern books or you could cut images from wrapping paper or magazines. Make sure that the paper for the images is fairly thin or you will create a ridged edge to the découpage, spoiling its smooth appearance.

The images must be cut out carefully with sharp scissors or a craft knife, glued in place with paper glue, and then varnished over several times to create the smooth, seamless finish of the best découpage.

For the botanical print used on these pages, a Victorian-style scrolled leaf pattern was used. Try to match the découpage form to that of the image you wish to frame, and also make sure it doesn't dominate the image. Use toning or dark colours for this purpose.

Checklist

Water-based paint (green)

Paintbrushes

Images for cutting out

Scissors, scalpel or craft knife

Paper glue

Sponge or soft cloth

Acrylic paints

Acrylic matt varnish

IMAGES FOR CUTTING OUT

SCISSORS

WATER-BASED PAINT

SOFT CLOTH

PAINTBRUSH

SCALPEL

PAPER GLUE

ACRYLIC PAINTS

PAINTBRUSH

TIP *Among good subjects for découpage are flowers, fruit, leaves, heraldic emblems, such as fleur-de-lis, and Greek and Roman ornament patterns.*

1 Paint the frame with a coat of water-based paint (in this case we used a dark green paint).

2 Cut out the images carefully using sharp scissors or a scalpel or craft knife. (If you are using either of the latter, you will need a suitable cutting board as well.)

3 Position the cut-out images on the frame, moving them about until you are happy with the arrangement. If necessary, trim any of the images to fit better.

4 Spread paper glue on the reverse of the images. Ensure that the glue gets to every small corner of the image.

TIP *If you wish, paint the images with a tinted wash before you cut them out. Tape the paper down with masking tape while you paint to prevent the paper from buckling. A good antiquing wash can be made from strong black coffee or tea.*

5 Smooth the images in place with a sponge or soft cloth so that the edges are stuck firmly and do not peel away. Allow to dry thoroughly.

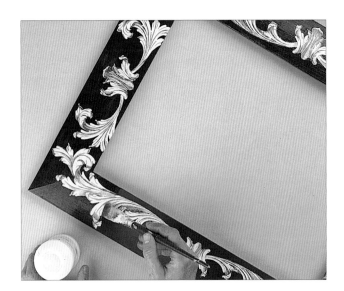

7 Apply a coat of acrylic varnish to the frame and allow to dry. Then repeat two or three times until a smooth even finish is obtained.

6 Paint the images with a little sepia or burnt umber acrylic wash for an antiqued appearance, or see the tip to the left. Allow to dry.

This botanical print of a tulip has been given a suitable treatment with scrolled acanthus leaves découpaged onto a dark green frame.

Chapter Five
SPECIAL FRAMING

*Certain objects you may wish to frame will demand
particular mounting and framing techniques. For example,
if the subject is three-dimensional, you may wish to create a
special mount for it, known as a shadow mount, with a
deeper than usual frame to emphasize its three-dimensional
attributes (see pages 104-9). Other subjects that need
special treatment are those that require stretching to avoid
buckling or warping if they are to look their best. These
include oil paintings on canvas and embroidery (see pages
115-18). Any item whose edge is a feature or an
integral part of the finished image will need to be mounted
in such a way that the edge is revealed (see pages 119-21).*

*Alternatively, you may wish to use a modern
aluminium frame rather than the traditional wooden kind
discussed so far in this book. These are put together using a
different technique; the way to use them is discussed
on pages 110-14.*

Making a Shadow Mount

When you want to frame any form of three-dimensional image – a picture made from pressed flowers or a woodcut, perhaps – you will need to use a deeper moulding, known as a box frame. Additionally, you could decide to set the work into a raised mount, creating a 'shadow effect'. This, too, needs a deeper than usual moulding to accommodate the thickness.

To create this raised mount, you will need special mounting board, known as foam core board. It comes in two thicknesses (5mm/¾in or 3mm/⅛in). You may need to put a couple of these together to achieve the desired depth for the subject being framed.

The foam core board is invisible once the image is correctly mounted so, if necessary, you can use remnants of core board to make up the shadow mount. First, measure the thickness of the image to be mounted, and then work out how many thicknesses of foam core board you will need to give an appropriate depth. For this image a depth of 9mm/⅜in was needed, and three thicknesses of 3mm/⅛in board were used. Ideally, the final thickness of the mount should be a fraction deeper than the subject, to ensure it clears it.

On pages 108-9 you can see how the frame containing the mount was stained. The finished project is shown on the opposite page.

Checklist

Image to be framed

Mount cards

Base board

Double-sided tape

Foam core board in two thicknesses

Straightedge

Craft knife

DOUBLE-SIDED TAPE

MOUNT CARDS

IMAGE TO BE FRAMED

FOAM CORE BOARD IN TWO THICKNESSES

The completed shadow mount, showing how the image recedes, the raised mount giving it a three-dimensional appearance. To frame it, a box frame with a deep moulding was used to accommodate the extra thickness.

TIP *Before you make the shadow mount, you will have to select appropriate coloured mount cards for the top mount and the under mount. In this case, a cream top mount with a pink under mount was selected to enhance the colour of the image in the centre. Instructions for making a double mount are shown on pages 26-9 (with a Cushway cutter) and also on pages 48-51 (with a Logan compact cutter).*

1 Cut a double mount out of standard mount card. Cut the backing board to the dimensions of the double mount. Then, on the back of the under mount, stick a strip of double-sided tape along each side, near to the aperture.

2 Work out the appropriate depth for the image, and then assemble the pieces of foam core board you will require – in this case, three pieces of 3mm/⅛in thick core board.

3 Cut the pieces of core board to the dimensions of the mount card (the width should be slightly narrower than the width of the mount border) using the straightedge and craft knife. Fasten double-sided tape to one side of each piece.

4 Stick the pieces of core board to each other and then to the base board. Check that the thickness of the shadow mount clears the central image.

These attractive flowers have been made from several layers of cut-out flower motifs, glued together to create a raised, three-dimensional image. When mounting items that are similarly delicate in hue, pick a mount card colour that harmonizes well, without overwhelming the subject.

Below: The shadow mounted image before being framed. Note how the double mount, raised away from the image, casts a delicate shadow on the base board, giving rise to its name.

5 Stick the image to the base board, and position the shadow mount over it. Once the mount is correctly positioned, stick it in place with double-sided tape.

Staining a Frame

To give a natural wood frame an interesting finish, you can stain it with a proprietary wood stain. Any natural wood frame can be stained, either to give it the colour of traditional hardwood, such as oak, mahogany or beech, for example, or in a more contemporary style in any one of a number of art shades. The stain, which is based on methylated spirits, simply creates a thin coloured coating on the wood, but being transparent, allows the grain of the wood to show through. When choosing a colour for staining, aim to find one that tones with the central image.

1 Apply the stain to the made-up frame using the soft-bristled paintbrush and allow to dry. Repeat if necessary with a second coat to obtain a deeper colour. Again, leave to dry.

Checklist

Plain wood frame

Wood stain

Paintbrush (soft-bristled)

Liming wax

Soft cloth or wire wool (fine-grade)

SOFT CLOTH

PLAIN WOOD FRAME

WOOD STAIN

PAINTBRUSH

LIMING WAX

2   Rub in the liming wax using either a fine-grade steel wool or soft cloth. Leave the wax for 15 minutes or so to dry.

3   Buff up the frame with the wire wool or soft cloth to remove any surplus wax and to create a smooth, polished surface.

TIPS If you do not have a Framemaster, you can tap nails into the moulding to hold the assembled frame in place.

If you wish to create paler, more opaque colours, or give the stained frame a more antiqued appearance, apply a coat of liming wax to the finish once it is dry. This will make it paler, more subtle and softer look-ing. In this case, a box frame in natural pine was stained in a deep red, which was then toned down to a soft pink using liming wax.

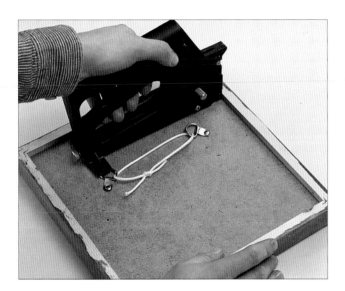

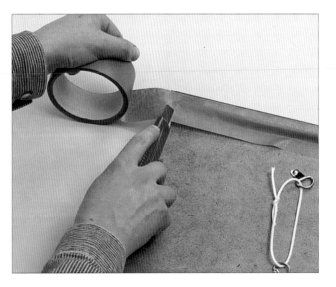

4   Insert the image and assemble in the usual way (see pages 42-4). Use a Framemaster to hold the image in place. Clip the assembled image into the rebate of the frame on the back.

5   Tape up the back of the picture with gummed paper tape (see page 45).

Framing a Poster

Large modern works of art, such as posters, black and white drawings or sizable photographs, for example, may well look better with a narrow aluminium frame rather than a traditional wooden one. You cannot cut aluminium with a standard mitre box and saw, but you can buy the aluminium ready-cut by the supplier to your own measurements.

Although you can frame a poster directly against the glass, if artwork is valuable you do not want it to touch the glass, as this can lead to staining or mottling. So for limited-edition prints or drawings, you may be better advised to mount the image first. For a poster or a simple drawing, such as this one, however, the float-mounting technique outlined overleaf works very well.

You will first need to measure the image, and stick it to the mount using acid-free tape. Then, having measured your image and ordered the extruded aluminium moulding to the appropriate cut lengths, the next task is to join them together and assemble the image in its frame. With aluminium frames, you need to make a similar allowance for 'ease' as you do for wooden mouldings, so add 2mm/⅛in to each of the desired measurements.

The frame comes supplied with cut lengths, corner plates, screws and spring clips ready to assemble.

This pencil drawing of a nude has been float-mounted on a toning mount card and framed with a narrow silver extruded aluminium frame.

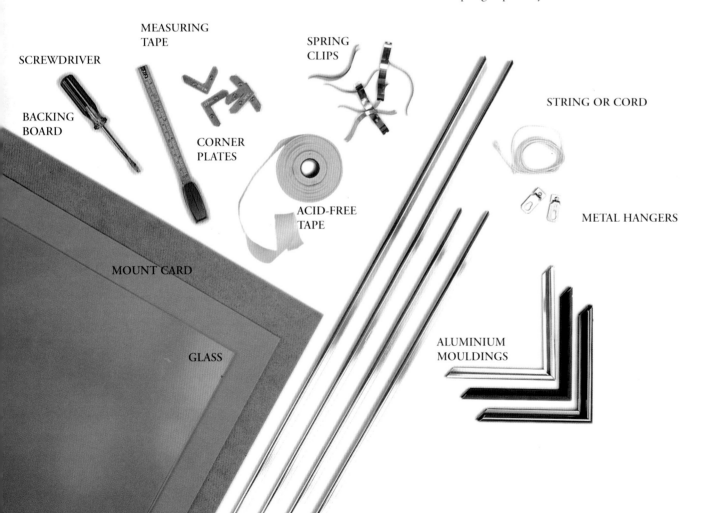

SCREWDRIVER

MEASURING TAPE

SPRING CLIPS

STRING OR CORD

BACKING BOARD

CORNER PLATES

ACID-FREE TAPE

METAL HANGERS

MOUNT CARD

GLASS

ALUMINIUM MOULDINGS

Checklist

Acid-free tape

Backing board

Measuring tape

Aluminium mouldings cut to length

Corner plates

Mount card

Glass

Metal hangers

Spring clips

String or cord

Craft knife

Screwdriver

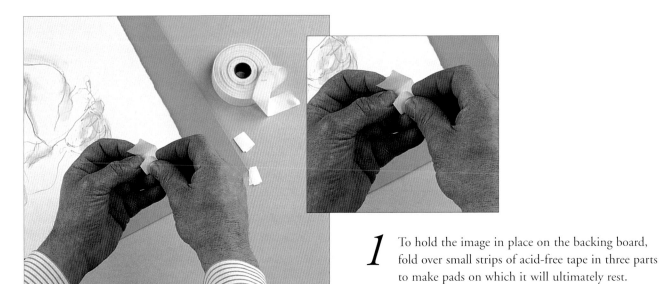

1 To hold the image in place on the backing board, fold over small strips of acid-free tape in three parts to make pads on which it will ultimately rest.

2 Centralize the image on the backing board. It is usual to have a deeper border at the base because when you are looking up at a picture this can improve the proportions. Then stick the pads to the backing board about 5cm/2in in from each corner of the image.

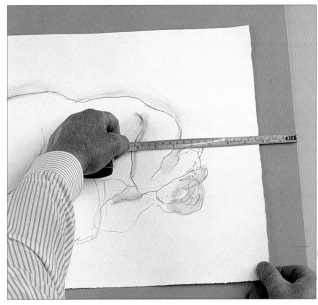

3 Position the image once again on the backing board, measuring the border to ensure that the top and two sides are the same so that the image is centrally positioned.

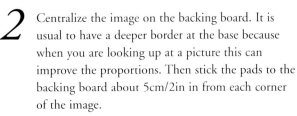

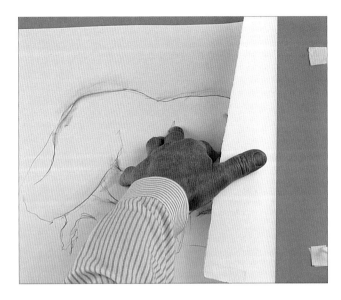

4 Wet the tabs to make them sticky and press the image down onto them to fix it.

5 To assemble the aluminium frame, push two lengths of the frame together at a time and screw a small plate into position at each corner. For now, prepare only two adjoining corners in this way.

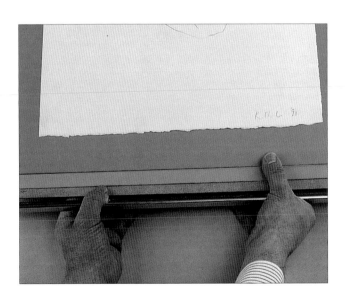

6 Assemble the backing board with the image, mount and glass (see page 45), and insert in the partly made-up frame.

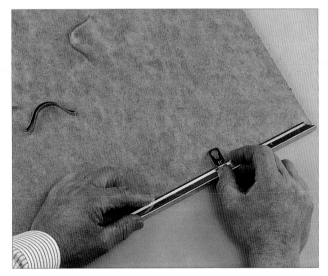

7 Add the hangers by slotting them into the edges on the reverse side of the frame, and then screw in the last two corners of the frame as described in step 5.

TIP *When you are assembling the image in the frame you will need to insert the spring clips between the frame and the backing board to hold it in place. The number of clips you use depends on the size of the frame, but you will normally need to insert them at 15cm/6in intervals.*

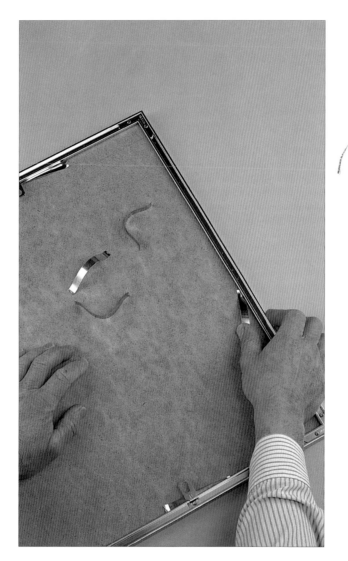

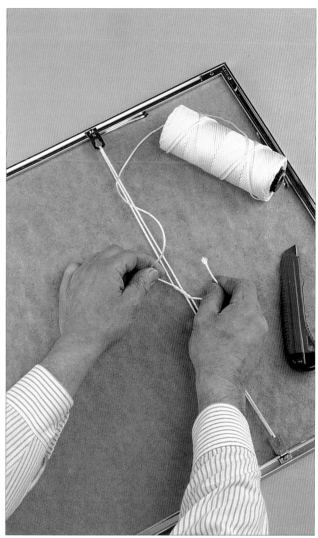

8 Insert the springs on each side of the frame between the frame and the backing board. These keep the backing board, mount and image tight within the frame.

9 Finally, thread the string through the hangers and tie in a triple knot. Your framed image is now ready to hang on the wall.

Framing an Oil Painting

If you paint in oils, you may well choose to buy your canvas by the roll and then stretch it yourself. Equally, if you acquire an oil painting, it may well be unstretched. Either way, before it is framed, the canvas needs to be stretched to ensure that it is taut.

Stretcher bars are made of cheap pine of a reasonable thickness with pre-cut mitred corners. Each mitred end has slots cut out to enable a section of each stretcher bar to dovetail with the other. Small wedges of wood (usually the pieces cut from the stretcher bar) are then tapped into the joints once the canvas is in place ensuring that the canvas (which is stapled or nailed over the the stretcher bars), is properly stretched and taut. The stretcher bars have a raised lip, over which the canvas is rolled; a flat edge can cut the canvas.

It is possible to make the stretchers yourself, but cutting the joints is tricky and time-consuming. So as the stretchers can be bought ready-cut to measure, it is probably simpler to miss out on the first task, and join together pre-cut stretchers. Because oil paintings have a reasonably permanent, wipeable finish, it is not normally necessary to use glass for protection. In fact, the sheen of the varnish coupled with reflections in the glass makes it difficult to see the painting properly, and as a consequence it is accepted practice to frame canvases without glass. That said, a very fragile oil painting of great value might well be safer behind glass, but inevitably if you have such a painting you will seek professional advice as to framing, anyway.

Checklist

4 stretcher bars

Hammer

Measuring tape

Staple gun

8 corner wedges

Ready-made frame with deep rebate

Z-clips

D-rings

String or cord

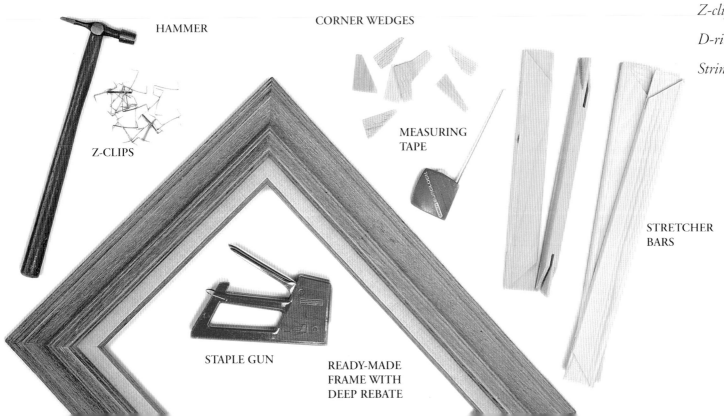

HAMMER

CORNER WEDGES

Z-CLIPS

MEASURING TAPE

STRETCHER BARS

STAPLE GUN

READY-MADE FRAME WITH DEEP REBATE

1 Gently push the stretcher bars together so that the mitred corners fit neatly. If necessary, tap the edges with a hammer to push them well in.

2 Check the frame is square by measuring from outside corner to outside corner. The measure should be the same across each diagonal, but if not, gently hammer the corners until the edges fit together properly.

3 Staple the canvas to the frame, as tightly as possible, fixing the two opposite central staples first, mid-way between the corners of the frame. Then staple from either side of each central staple towards the corners.

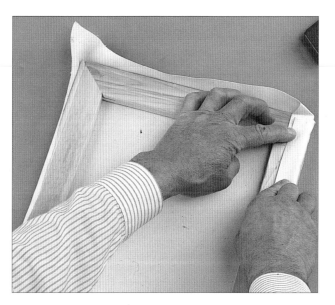

4 Fold the corners over neatly on the back of the stretcher by folding first one side down and then the other over it. Then staple the corners in position, making sure you do not pin across the corners.

Opposite: After stretching, this oil landscape was framed in a broad, grey-stained moulding sympathetic to the colours in the painting. Framing an oil painting without glass allows the surface texture of the paint to be appreciated.

TIP *When you stretch a canvas on stretcher bars it is important to ensure even tautness, so start stapling at the middle of each pair of opposite sides, making a central 'cross' of stretched canvas. Then staple outwards from the cross to the corners. In this way you are stretching the canvas out smoothly from the centre to the edges.*

5 Push two of the wedges into each corner (flat edge to flat edge) to keep the canvas as taut as possible. When all eight wedges are in place, tap them lightly, making sure you tap each corner in turn to maintain an even stretch.

6 Take the frame you intend to use, and tap the Z-clips into the inner part of the frame with the hammer. Use at least two Z-clips to a long side and one to each short side.

7 Insert the painting, face down, and turn over the Z-clips to hold it in position. Then hammer them down through the back of the stretchers. If you are using a backing board, fix the D-rings to this. But if not, they can be fixed to the back of the frame, particularly if, as here, there is an inner and outer part of the frame.

Framing a Textile

*If you are framing a textile, you will need to stretch
it before it is framed, but the stretching method will
depend on the kind of textile involved: whether it is
flat cloth or canvaswork. Likewise, the frame you
choose will depend on the nature of the embroidery,
but in general try to pick a style that is sympathetic
to the period and form of the embroidery or tapestry.*

Whether or not you use a mount will be determined by the
embroidery itself, and also by personal preference. The
advantage of a mount is that it keeps the glass away from the
textile, avoiding any possible damage.

When stretching any textile, it is important to work from
the centre points of each edge and move towards the corners.
This ensures an even stretch across the centre of the textile
without any danger of puckering the fabric.

FLOAT-MOUNTING A TEXTILE

Textiles with a firm cloth background, like the embroidered
Afghan cushion overleaf, can be float-mounted on a card
base and pinned and stitched in place. This method of display is ideal for a textile that has an attractive edging that
you do not want to lose, as you would if you stretched it
over stretcher bars (see Stretching Canvaswork on page 120).

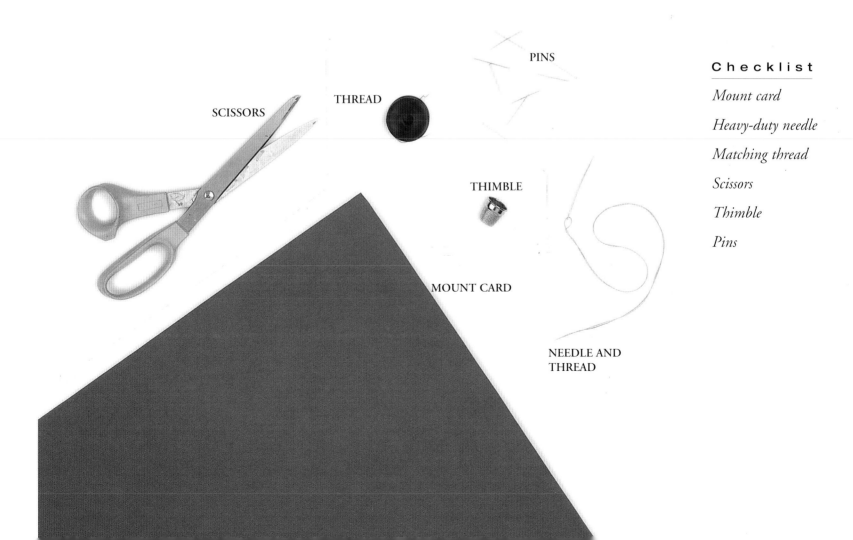

PINS

THREAD

SCISSORS

THIMBLE

MOUNT CARD

NEEDLE AND
THREAD

Checklist

Mount card

Heavy-duty needle

Matching thread

Scissors

Thimble

Pins

Opposite: The stretched Afghan cushion has been float-mounted on a toning mount card. A traditional wooden frame was chosen as an appropriate finish.

1 Measure the stretched textile and cut a piece of mount card with an allowance for a border. Pin the textile in position, first taking care to pin the centre point of each edge.

2 Using a heavy-duty needle, stitch the textile to the mount card. Take small, invisible stitches at the edge of the textile, pushing the needle to the back of the card. Then work outwards towards each corner, working on opposite sides in turn.

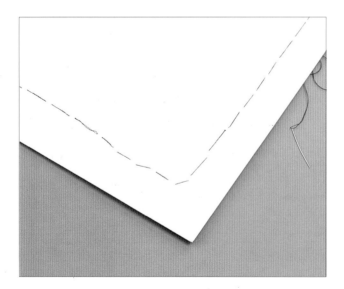

3 You can make larger stitches (roughly 2cm/⅜in each) on the reverse. Frame as usual.

STRETCHING CANVASWORK

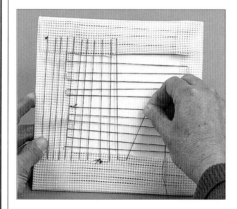

Counted thread work, done on canvas, will need to be stretched properly before it is framed to ensure that it is square, as the canvas easily pulls out of true. The best means of doing this is to lace the canvas on the back, having first created an appropriately sized stretcher for it (see page 117) or use strong card. You will need a fairly stout needle and strong thread. Turn the canvas over the stretcher, and work across the back of the canvas, pulling the opposite sides firmly together. On a canvas of any size, work across the centre first and then out towards the outer edges.

Chapter Six
NOVELTY FRAMES AND MOUNTS

In this section, various finishes are featured using different materials or techniques to create the decoration to the frame or mount. There is no limit to the styles and materials you can choose, and it often pays to look around for unusual materials for frames: for example, in place of the silver foil used in the embossed frame (see pages 124-7), you could use fabric, stuck in a similar manner to the frame itself. Alternatively, pressed flowers or seashells could be glued to the frame. The simple cardboard frame on pages 132-4 is very easy and cheap to make, but not particularly durable. Another version could be made from painted hardboard, for example, or any other rigid, but cuttable, material you might have to hand.

Silver Foil Embossing

You can use a wide variety of simple patterns for embossing, but geometric designs are the most straightforward if you have little skill as a freehand artist. Ideally, the embossed design should reflect the central image in some way. Among the easiest designs are simple triangles, stars and ladder motifs. Alternatively, you could use a coin to make circles.

The foil that you need for this embossed aluminium frame should be of a heavier gauge than that normally used for cooking. It is usually available from art suppliers, in silver, brass and copper colours. The decoration requires very little skill or equipment – all you need is an old biro or blunt pencil – and it will give a new lease of life to any old or damaged frame. Ideally, however, the frame base should be flat and fairly wide to enable you to carry out the embossing successfully.

The foil is very soft, and while this makes the embossing easy, it also means that it can easily get marked or damaged, so work on the frame with care. Take care not to press so hard that the instrument cuts through the foil. Once made, store the frame carefully until it is ready to be hung, taking care no heavy objects are placed on top of it.

Checklist

Silver aluminium foil (heavy gauge)

Flat wooden frame

Scissors

Blunt pencil

Straightedge

Notepad

All-purpose adhesive

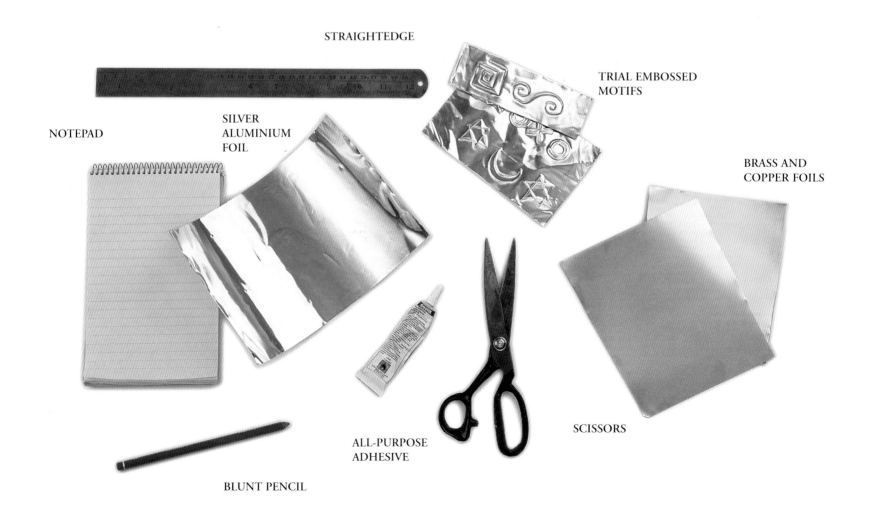

STRAIGHTEDGE

TRIAL EMBOSSED MOTIFS

NOTEPAD

SILVER ALUMINIUM FOIL

BRASS AND COPPER FOILS

ALL-PURPOSE ADHESIVE

SCISSORS

BLUNT PENCIL

1 Cut two pieces of foil to cover the top and bottom of the frame. Make them long enough to cover the width of the frame and the sides, and wide enough to cover the front, aperture, outside edges and for a turning onto the back. Notch the aperture corners.

2 Cut two pieces long enough to cover the sides of the frame (less the depth of the top and base), and of equal width to the top and bottom pieces. Position them on each edge of the frame, and notch in each corner of the aperture.

3 To determine the area to be decorated, apply the foil to the top and bottom of the frame, turn it over, and mark the edge of the frame with a pencil.

4 Using the straightedge, make a lip for each of the horizontal bands of foil where they cover the aperture.

5 Place the foil face down on a fairly soft surface such as a note pad, and emboss any kind of regular geometric design with a biro or blunt pencil (anything too sharp will rip the foil). Repeat for all four sides of the frame.

6 To fasten the decorated foil bands to the frame, apply adhesive to the points of the frame where the edges of the foil will be positioned, such as the inside of the aperture. Glue on the side strips first.

7 Be careful not to flatten the raised embossed pattern when applying the other two sides. Cut the foil to fold around the corners.

8 Clip and glue the final corners to the back of the frame, to finish it off neatly on the reverse side. As a final touch, burnish the corners with a blunt tool.

The embossed silver
aluminium foil frame
surrounds a mirror,
giving it a pleasing
modern appearance.
A simple repeating
pattern, like the one
here, is easy to carry out
and looks effective.

Gilding and Antiquing

There are many ways of gilding, some of which require considerable skill to produce a good result. Using gold leaf, as shown overleaf, is easy and quick, but the gold leaf is not particularly cheap, and is therefore probably best used for smaller frames.

The leaf is available in gold, silver and copper. It is supplied between sheets of tissue paper, and must be stored carefully until required.

Before you apply the gold (or copper or silver) leaf, you need to paint the frame with goldsize, to which it will adhere. If the leaf breaks up as you use it, do not worry. The pieces can be patched and overlapped if necessary, creating an attractive antiqued finish.

If you use a dark coloured base coat under the gold or silver leaf and then rub the applied leaf with wire wool afterwards, you will reveal some of the base coat, giving the frame a suitably antique finish. When handling gold leaf, dust your hands first with talcum powder to prevent the gold leaf sticking to them.

The warm glow of the antiqued, burnished copper leaf covering this decorative frame perfectly complements the style and tonal values of the image (a print of a drawing by François Boucher).

Checklist

Sandpaper

Emulsion paint (blue-black)

Paintbrushes (flat, soft)

Acrylic goldsize

Talcum powder

Copper leaf (or silver or gold leaf)

Soft cloth

Wax (Georgian mahogany)

Wire wool (fine grade)

WIRE WOOL

SOFT CLOTH

DARK-COLOURED WAX

SANDPAPER

COPPER LEAF

SILVER LEAF

GOLD LEAF

EMULSION PAINT

ACRYLIC GOLDSIZE

PAINTBRUSH

TIP *If you want to try different colours of base coat beneath the gold or silver leaf, you could opt for a dark bottle green or maybe a deep chestnut colour, or a burgundy. Much depends on the style and colour of the central image and the colour of the leaf.*

1 If necessary, sand down the frame with medium-weight sandpaper to remove any old varnish.

2 Apply the base coat (here the blue-black emulsion paint). Coat it on liberally. You do not need to apply this coat particularly carefully as it will be covered by gold leaf, and only parts will show through later.

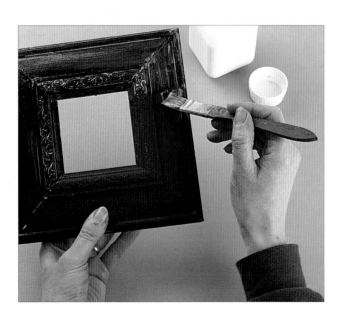

3 After it has dried, cover the frame with acrylic gold-size using a soft paintbrush. Then leave to dry once again.

4 Dust your hands with talcum powder to remove grease and then take sheets of loose copper leaf one by one and lay them over the frame, patching them on. Push them well into the edges of the moulding.

5 Once the copper leaf is roughly in place, smooth it down lightly with a cloth to ensure that the edges of the copper leaf stick down securely.

6 Apply Georgian mahogany wax with the fine wire wool. The waxing will remove some of the copper sheets and give the frame more of an antiqued look.

7 Leave to dry for 15 minutes and then burnish once more with the soft cloth.

Making a Corrugated Paper Frame

If you have a simple image to frame, such as this small collage, or perhaps a still-life of leaves and twigs, you could create a similarly 'natural' frame using corrugated paper. Even old boxes can be recycled for this purpose, but coloured corrugated paper, bought from an art supplier, makes an attractive frame. Try to find a suitably coloured corrugated paper to echo one of the colours in your image.

This very basic frame is relatively easy to make, but you will need a craft knife with a very sharp blade to ensure that the cardboard does not tear when you cut it. Make sure that you also have a suitably firm cutting board on which to cut the cardboard.

The cardboard frame here includes a small rebate to allow glass to be included in the final assembly. The image itself can either be float-mounted as here, or mounted with a single or double mount, as shown earlier.

Do not expect this frame to be very durable: it is for fun rather than for displaying a valuable subject.

Checklist

Straightedge

Pencil

Set square

Cardboard (heavy duty)

PVA adhesive

Craft knife

Coloured corrugated board

Glass

Natural string or twine

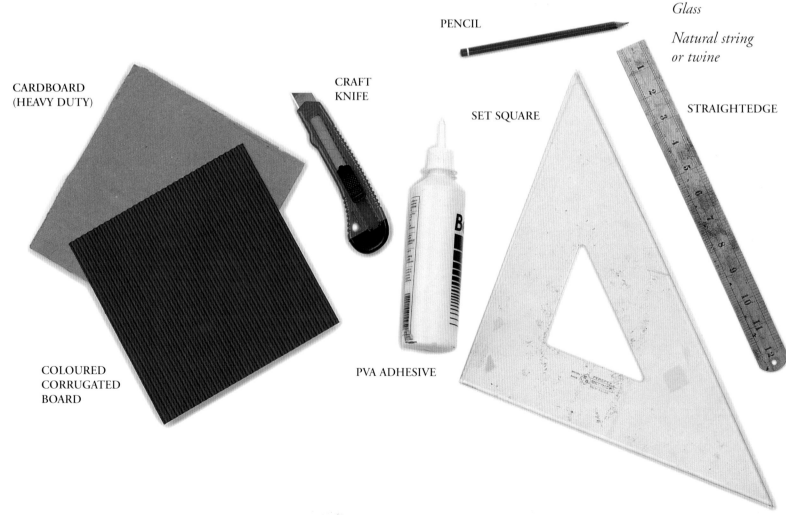

CARDBOARD (HEAVY DUTY)

CRAFT KNIFE

PENCIL

SET SQUARE

STRAIGHTEDGE

COLOURED CORRUGATED BOARD

PVA ADHESIVE

The finished cardboard frame has been used to surround a small decorative fabric collage. This quick and easy, inexpensive style of frame is ideal for informal or ephemeral images.

1 Measure the image and then decide on the size of the final frame. First cut the frame base (the heavy duty cardboard) to the appropriate measurements, using a set square to ensure that it is square.

2 To mark the area for the aperture, draw two diagonal lines between the opposite corners of the cut board, and rule off an appropriate width of frame, adding 5mm/⅓₁₆in all around to allow for a rebate.

3 Cut the card to remove the aperture area. Then cut the covering coloured corrugated cardboard to the appropriate size but without adding the rebate allowance around the aperture. Glue the cardboard frame to the back of the corrugated frame

To finish the picture, once you have made the simple corrugated frame, float-mount the central image on a piece of card cut to fit the rebate. Tape the backing card to the back of the frame and staple a length of string to the back with which to hang the picture.

PRACTICAL INFORMATION

Included in this section are instructions on hanging pictures correctly, together with advice on how to look after them and on carrying out minor repairs. We also give a glossary of the terms used in this book and a list of useful suppliers for the various items of equipment you will need before you start to frame pictures.

Hanging a Picture

Having successfully framed your pictures, it is important to hang them properly and securely. There are various ways in which you can do this, but the easiest is described here.

There are a number of different kinds of picture hooks you can use, ranging from the traditional X-hooks to the more modern plastic, pin fittings. The former are generally used for nailing into plaster, the latter for such surfaces as brick-work on which normal strength picture nails would bend. If the wall surface is very hard you may need to drill a hole and use a Rawlplug and screw to hang the picture.

It is particularly important when hanging pictures in groups to fix the nails so that the pictures hang precisely where you want them. The best solution is to turn the picture over, pull the string taut in the centre and measure the distance from the taut string to the top of the frame. If you measure down from the point on the wall where you want the top of the frame to come by this distance you will be able to see clearly where to position the nail. Make sure you use strong enough string or cord to take the weight of the frame. Heavy pictures may be safer if hung with picture wire rather than string or cord.

1 With a pencil, mark the position of the top line of the frame on the wall. Measure the width of the picture and mark this on the wall, too. Then mark the central point of this distance where it meets the top line mark.

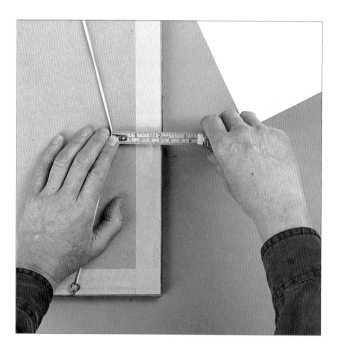

2 Turn the picture over, pull the string or cord taut in the centre, and measure from this point to the top of the frame.

3 Measure down from your pencil mark on the wall to this measurement, and mark it on the wall. This is the point at which you will hammer the nail into the wall.

 Fix the nail into the wall, by hammering it in lightly. If you are using a picture hook, position the hook at the distance from the taut string to the top of the frame and mark where the nail is to go above it at the appropriate point, i.e. the nail will be higher up the wall.

5 Hang the picture, and then adjust it afterwards, by eye or with a spirit level, to ensure it is straight.

TIP *If you are hanging a group of pictures, you may have to make a decision whether to keep the tops or the bases level, if the pictures are of different sizes. Practise first laying the pictures out on a table, or on the floor, to see which arrangement looks the most balanced and the most effective. In a small group, put the largest picture in the centre, with smaller pictures flanking it.*

Problem Solving

Occasionally you may need to do some repair and restoration work to get your pictures into a presentable condition. Obviously, any major restoration work on a valuable image should be handled by a professional restorer, but there are a number of useful tips and techniques for removing minor flaws and blemishes when mounting or framing works of art.

Remove the image from the frame, and check whether the marks are on the glass, the mount, or the image itself. If the glass only is dirty, remove it from the frame, clean it and reassemble the image. If the glass is old and scratched, replace it. If the mount is marked or damaged, remove that, and make a new one.

Condensation or damp can cause problems, making marks on the mount and even on the central image. If the mount has become mottled (known as foxing), then use an acid-free conservation quality mount card next time around. Foxing on a work of art on paper needs professional restoration, but if the image is damaged in other ways, look carefully to see if there are any tears, dirty marks or blemishes towards the edge, they could be covered with a larger mount than previously used. If so, then opt for this as the first choice. However, if you can't follow this course, look to see if you can remove the problem. In the case of a photograph with a crease or bend, you may well be able to minimize the problem by dry mounting the image. By glueing it to a backing board you will help remove the crease, and you can further reduce this by burnishing it with a blunt instrument (see right and opposite).

Oil paintings can be cleaned quite simply, usually by using a dampened rag. Dirt that is harder to remove should be cleaned by a professional picture cleaner as you risk removing some of the pigment as well if you use any proprietary cleaning fluids.

Avoiding Problems

Try to hang valuable images out of direct sunlight as in many cases this will cause the image to fade unevenly. Nor should you hang anything valuable in kitchens or bathrooms, where humidity is high – it will cause both the image and the mounting materials to buckle and warp, and you may get mould or condensation marks as well. Try to ensure that the images are not over a heat source, such as a radiator, which will cause glue to dry out, and varnish to crack.

There are various ways in which you can deal with damaged frames. If a simple wooden frame is scratched, you could either sand it down or, if you prefer, you could decorate the frame using one of the ways suggested earlier in this book. Painting or antiquing the frame would be ideal methods of disguising blemishes. Small holes can be filled with wood filler, sanded and the frame then stained or painted.

Maintaining Frames

Periodically, check your pictures for signs of wear and tear. Remove the picture from its backing, clean the glass and replace any broken or peeled pieces of gummed tape with new tape. Make sure all hooks are firmly fixed into the wall, and that the string or wire is securely fixed to the picture.

If in any doubt as to the value or the requirements of a particular image, seek proper professional help from a reputable picture restorer.

Removing a Crease from a Photograph

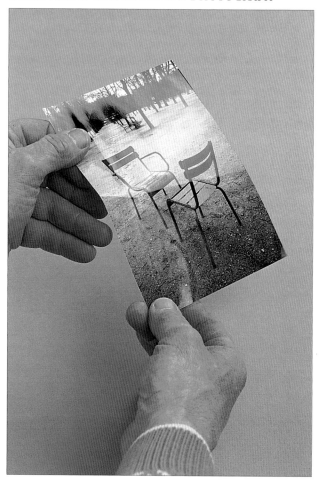

1 This photograph was badly marked with heavy creases which would have been clearly visible when the picture was framed.

A heavily marked crease marred this photographic print. Although the crease could not be totally removed, by the time the print was mounted and framed, the crease was almost invisible, thanks to this simple mounting technique. This is an acceptable solution provided the print is not valuable.

2 Cut a piece of sticky-backed paper to the same size as the mount. Lay the mount over the paper and mark the four corners of the aperture with a pin to show where to position your print. Peel off the backing sheet.

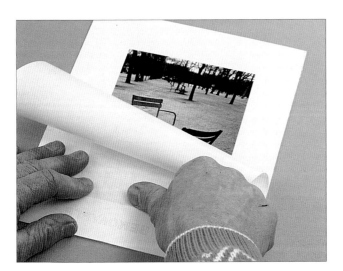

3 Position the photograph onto the sticky surface using the pin holes for guidance. Burnish out the creases with a blunt tool over the backing sheet, then press lightly with your thumb over the whole picture to smooth it.

4 Now place the mount carefully over the print and press down firmly onto the sticky paper.

GLOSSARY

ACID-FREE
Term used to describe mount card and board that has a pH value of 7.5 to 9 per cent. Used for valuable images. Papers that contain acid can damage the image with which they are in contact.

BEVEL
An angled cut, usually at 45 degrees. Used generally to describe the angle of the cut of a mount card or a moulding.

BOX FRAME
A deeper than usual frame used to display three-dimensional pieces of art-work.

BRADAWL
A pointed hand tool used for initially piercing a hole in wood to receive screws or nails.

CLIP FRAME
A simple hardboard and glass frame, held together with metal clips.

CONSERVATION BOARD
High quality acid- and chemical-free board used for framing valuable works of art.

DÉCOUPAGE
The technique of creating a decorated surface using cut-out pieces of paper, which are glued and then varnished to the surface.

DOUBLE MOUNT
Two mounts used together to create a decorative effect, the top mount having a larger window than the under mount, which is then revealed in the aperture, in whatever width is required, but normally around 5mm/³⁄₁₆in.

FLOAT MOUNTING
A technique whereby the back of the image is lightly taped to the backing card, revealing the natural edge of the central image.

FOXING
Yellowish brown mottled marks on an image or mount caused by mildew.

GLASS CUTTER
Special tool for glass cutting. Most basic types have a rotary wheel which is pressed against the glass, scoring it so that it can then be broken cleanly.

FRAMEMASTER
Tool that fires metal darts into a moulding to secure the assembled elements.

GLAZE
A layer of varnish applied as a finish.

GLAZING GUN
(see FRAMEMASTER)

HINGE MOUNT
Form of hinge used to float mount art on board.

LIMING
Technique of applying lime (in the form of a wax or paste) to wood in order to bleach it.

MARBLED PAPER
Paper that has been given a surface pattern resembling the veins of marble by being dragged (by hand or machine) through a bath of pigmented oils in water.

MITRE
The angled join of two pieces of moulding, both cut at a 45-degree angle, that makes a neatly fitting corner.

MITRE BOX AND SAW
A tool that enables you to cut mitres efficiently.

MOULDING
The technical term for the wooden pieces that create the frame. Can be cut, embossed or decorated in a range of styles.

MOUNT (MAT)
The surround to an image, laid over it. Materials used for mounting can be cards of varying types and thicknesses, or other materials such as fabric.

MULTI-CUTTER
A tool containing several blades that can cut several strips of paper to the same width at one time.

REBATE
The inner, stepped, part of a moulding into which the subject, glass and mount are fitted.

RULING PEN
Special tool for creating decorative lines on a mount. It is charged with ink or watercolour.

SCORE
To create a partly cut line in board or glass, for example, which can then be broken cleanly and easily by pressure alone.

SLIP
(see UNDER MOUNT)

STRETCHER
The wooden frame on which a canvas is stretched. It has specially-made corners, with cut-out parts, so that wedges can be inserted to create greater pressure to make the stretched material (usually the canvas on which oil paintings are executed) taut.

UNDER MOUNT
The inner (or under) mount used in a double mount to reveal a second narrow border around the aperture. (Also called SLIP.)

V-GROOVE
A decorative cut line, with two angled cuts, one on the top surface of the card, the other on the reverse, that together make a distinctive, decorative cut in the mount. Usually executed on card with a contrasting coloured inner core.

WASH LINE
Wash between two ruled lines applied as a decoration to a mount card. It usually has additional ruled lines along either side.

SUPPLIERS

UNITED KINGDOM
Ademco Ltd
12-13 Blenheim Road
Cressex Industrial Estate
High Wycombe
Bucks HP12 3RS
Tel: 01494 448661

Aluminium Framing
Supplies
40-44 Peel Road
London E18 2LG
Tel: 0181 505 3434

Arquati (UK) Ltd
2 Wolseley Road
Kempston
Bedford
MK42 7AY
Tel: 01234 857488

Ashworth & Thompson Ltd
Freeston Drive
Blenheim Industrial Estate
Bulwell
Nottingham
Tel: 01602 278504

Byron Mouldings
Ashley Industrial Estate
East
Bradley Junction
Leeds Road
Huddersfield
HD2 1UR
Tel: 01484 434874

Charisma School of
Framing
57-59 Station Road
Harrow
Middlesex HA1 2TY
Tel: 0181 863 8257

Concorde Glass Ltd
Concorde House
Caxton Street North
London E16 1JL
Tel: 0171 473 2791

L Cornelissen
105 Great Russell Street
London WC1B 3RY
Tel: 0171 636 1045

Croxley Framers' Supplies
3 Penn Place
Rickmansworth
Herts WD3 1RE
Tel: 01923 778189

D & J Simons & Sons Ltd
122-128 Hackney Road
London E2
Tel: 0171 739 3744

D & W Art Products
Edwin Avenue
Hoo Farm Industrial
Estate
Kidderminster
Worcs DY11 7RA
Tel: 01562 747355

Daler Framing
Peacock Lane
Bracknell
Berks
RG12 4ST
Tel: 01344 862055

Euro Mouldings Ltd
Decoy Road
Worthing
Sussex
BN14 8JH
Tel: 01903 205825

Framers' Corner
1-3 Rowan Street
Fosse Road North
Leicester LE3 9GP
Tel: 01533 511550

Framers' Equipment Ltd
Unit 3, Well Lane
Danbury
Essex CM3 4AD
Tel: 01245 415904

Hang-it Framing Systems
Ltd
225 Greenwich High Road
London SE10 4EF
Tel: 0181 858 2312

Lion Picture Framing
Supplies
148 Garrison Street
Bordesley
Birmingham B9 4BN
Tel: 0121 773 1230

Meridian Mouldings Ltd
The Old Maltings
Lombard Street
Orston
Notts NG13 9NG
Tel: 01949 50585

Priory Mouldings
North House
Ravensmere
Beccles
Suffolk NR34 9BE
Tel: 01502 714324

James Robinson Ltd
97 Lea Bridge Road
London E10 7QR
Tel: 0181 558 9340

for details of your nearest
stockist
Sisslings (Mouldings) Ltd
Merrydale Road
Euroway Estate
Bradford
West Yorks BD4 6SD
Tel: 01274 685353

Slater Harrison & Co Ltd
Lower House Mills
Bollington
Macclesfield SK10 5HW
Tel: 01625 573155

Sullivans Mouldings Ltd
Unit 1, Acorn Trading Estate
Gumley Road
West Thurrock
Essex RM16 1EP
Tel: 01375 380432

UK Mouldings Ltd
Framers House
Lanrick Road
London E14 0JF
Tel: 0181 987 5206

UNITED STATES
Aluminum Frame &
Extrusion Corp
18 Commerce Road
Fairfield
NJ 07004
Tel: (800) 524 0583

Art Essentials of New
York Ltd
Three Cross Road
Suffern
NY 10901
Tel: (913) 368 1100

Art Materials, Frames &
Moulding Co Inc
PO Box 5265
1205 Putman Drive NW
Huntsville
AL 35816
Tel: (205) 837 9710

DC Framing Supply
2443 South Curry Street
Carson City
NV 89703
Tel: (702) 882 8511

Frame & Art Depot
6479F Peachtree Ind. Blvd.
Atlanta
GA 30360
Tel: (404) 457 7131

Janow Wholesale Frame Inc
17 Andover Drive
West Hartford
CT 06110
Tel: (203) 953 9662

Kansas City Moulding
9343 West 74th Street
Shawnee Mission
KS 66204
Tel: (913) 432 3800

Lamarche Moulding Co
20780 Leapwood Ave
Carson
CA90746
Tel: (213) 515 0011

New England Frame Crafters
PO Box 814, King Court
Keene
NH 03431
Tel: (603) 357 4614

Northcoast Frame Supply
2479 Russell Street
Cuyahoga Falls
OH 44221
Tel: (216) 923 6144

PB & H Moulding Co
124 Pickard Drive East
Syracuse
NY 13211
Tel: (315) 455 5602

Presto Frame & Moulding
5 Diamond Avenue
Bethel
CT 06801
Tel: (203) 744 4499

Print Mount Co, Inc
204 Hartford Avenue
Providence
RI 02909
Tel: (401) 351 5480

Regal Frames, Inc
16520 Cincennes Road
South Holland
IL 60473
Tel: (312) 596 5400

S & W Framing Supplies
120 Broadway
Garden City Park
NY 11040
Tel: (516) 746 1000

Southern Moulding &
Supply Co
129 Armour Drive NE
Atlanta
GA 30324
Tel: (404) 872 0775

Stewart Moulding &
Frame Co
11500 Rojas Drive
El Paso

TX 79936
Tel: (915) 595 1898

TC Moulding & Supply
1901 Oakcrest Avenue
St Paul
MN 55113
Tel: (612) 636 6646

Zorba Frame & Moulding
29 Marne Street
Hamden
CT 06514
Tel: (203) 281 1111

AUSTRALIA
Art Barns of Australia
192 Newell Street
Westcourt, Cairns
Queensland 4870
Tel: 070 54 6555

Frames Equipment Co
50 Rooks Road
Nunawading
Victoria 3131
Tel: 03 872 3600

Gary McLean Framing
Supplies
34-36 Canterbury Road
Heathmont
Victoria 3135
Tel: 03 720 6405

Hughes Mouldings
37 UnwinStreet
Moorooka
Queensland 4195
Tel: 07 848 0126

Kosnar Framing
Equipment & Supplies
550 Mt Alexander Road
Ascot Vale
Victoria 3032
Tel: 03 370 5044

Mattboard
115 Highbury Road
Burwood
Victoria 3125
Tel: 03 888 8225

Timber Detail Mouldings
16-18 Sammut Street
Smithfield
NSW 2164
Tel: 02 604 6900

NEW ZEALAND
Art Picture Framers
502 Mt Eden Road
Mt Eden
Tel: (09) 688 961

Avon Picture Mouldings Ltd
142 Carlyle Street
Sydenham
Christchurch
Tel: (03) 667 060

Eastern Picture Framing Ltd
Cnr Kohlmarama Road
and Allurn Street
Kohlmarama
Tel: (09) 567 398

Focus Frame Centre
716 Dominion Road
Balmoral
Tel: (09) 604 428

The Frame Workshop
128 Ponsonby Road
Ponsonby
Tel: (09) 789 100

Kents Framers Ltd
170 Parnell Road
Parnell
Tel: (09) 393 821

Kwikframe
4132 The Concourse

Henderson
Tel: (09) 837 2606

Picture Moulding
Distributing Co Ltd
29 Ward Street
Dunedin
Tel: (024) 477 0492

Pictures and Frames
11 Cook Street
Howick
Tel: (09) 535 9467

INSTITUTES
The Fine Art Trade Guild
16-18 Empress Place
London SW6 1TT
UK
Tel: 0171 381 6616

Professional Picture
Framers' Association
4305 Sarellen Road
PO Box 7655
Richmond
VA 23231
USA
Tel: (804) 226 0430

The Australian Picture
Framers' Association Ltd
c/o The President
19 Glenferrie Avenue
Cremorne
NSW 2090
Australia

INDEX

ACKNOWLEDGMENTS

*The authors would like to thank the following for their help with this book:
the staff at Charisma, in particular Lin Boyall for decorating mounts and general advice
and also Claire Stubbings; Justine Faram for help at photography sessions; Kate Pollard
and Leeann Mackenzie for creating frames and Leeann also for styling; Michael Crockett
for his photography; Carol McCleeve for her design work; Emma Callery for editorial
work; and the team at Phoebus Editions for project management and general
help and support.*